OUTWARD BOUND
ROCK CLIMBING
HANDBOOK

Bob Barton

WARD LOCK

To Alex, Eliane and Flora

Acknowledgements

I would like to thank the staff of Outward Bound Eskdale, especially Bruce Poll, Tony Shepherd, Carol Emmons and Steve Prior for helpful comments, Moira Briggs and Alyson Carradice for painstaking secretarial support and Simon Greening for assistance with the illustrations. I am grateful to Allen, Jon, Harold, Keith, Sam, Dave, Brian and many others for memorable days on (and off!) the crags.

The support and encouragement given by Anna Barton have been as important to the completion of this book as they have been to the completion of many climbs.

A WARD LOCK BOOK
First published in the UK in 1995
by Ward Lock
Wellington House
125 Strand
London WC2R 0BB

A Cassell Imprint

Distributed in Australia by
Capricorn Link (Australia) Pty Ltd
213 Carrington Road, Castle Hill, NSW 2154

British Library Cataloguing-in-Publication data
A catalogue record for this book is available from the British Library

ISBN 0-7063-7364-2

Line illustrations: Tony Randell

Front cover photograph: Stephen Whitehorne

Back cover photograph: Mark Allen Publishing

Typesetting and design: Ben Cracknell

Printed and bound in Finland by Werner Söderström Oy

Contents

About Outward Bound®

The Outward Bound Trust provides high quality courses in a range of exciting outdoor activities. Our fully-qualified instructors maintain the highest standards of tuition, and our safety record is second to none. Everyone who takes an Outward Bound course enjoys a rewarding and memorable experience, the benefits of which will last a lifetime.

Outward Bound courses have been available in Britain since 1941. The original courses were the outcome of a meeting between Kurt Hahn, the educator, and Lawrence Holt, the owner of a shipping line. The marriage of the worlds of education and business is a vital feature of the Outward Bound movement. The courses are both a valuable adjunct to formal education and an important part of career development.

From its beginnings in Britain the Outward Bound movement has spread throughout the world, with 38 centres in 23 countries.

A typical course in the UK lasts from one to three weeks and may be based at one of our five national centres or take the form of an expeditionary journey by foot or by sailing boat in a wilderness setting. We run courses for all age groups, from 14 to 70!

The Outward Bound Trust also works directly with industry in designing programmes to help companies through periods of change. This may involve developing leadership skills for young managers or assisting in building cohesive teams. The courses balance challenging outdoor tasks with reflection and review. They are specially designed so that participants can always translate what they gain from a course back to their working environment.

After an Outward Bound experience, people discover many positive attributes about themselves. They become more confident; they learn to share, to lead and to follow, to understand their own strengths and to work together as a group. By safeguarding each other, they form bonds of trust. They discover that many problems can be solved only with the co-operation of all members of a group.

To find out more about Outward Bound courses or to request a brochure, please contact us at Outward Bound Trust, PO Box 1219, Windsor, Berkshire SL4 LXR, Tel. (01753) 731005

Michael Hobbs
Outward Bound Trust

1

Introduction

Sometimes it is best not to look down. We were following a tenuous line of cracks up the smooth granite walls of the unclimbed south-west pillar of a 6600m (21600ft) peak in the Garwhal Himalaya. This was Bhagirathi 3 and months of preparation and days of continuous climbing had brought us to this point, which seemed the realization of any rock climber's dream. The only line of weakness in the mountain's defences had led us out from shadowed, ice-filled cracks onto golden, sun-warmed granite at the edge of a huge monolithic corner. Below us the sweep of rock dropped uninterrupted to the Gangotri Glacier 1500m (4900ft) below; above was only the corner system, the summit and the sky. We moved slowly, like ants on a cathedral, but we were, against the odds, moving upwards.

Allen joined me on the tiny ledge where I half-stood, half-hung from the ropes and then moved past to push the route forward – a horizontal fault-line, invisible from below, allowing us to cross the smooth walls from our crack system to the huge corner.

The moment had everything: the close partnership of two people on the rope, uncertainty resolved and challenge met, and the absorbing technicalities of difficult climbing, all set against the backdrop of one of the most impressive mountain panoramas in the world. One of the delights of long rock climbs is the rhythm as pitch succeeds pitch; intense action followed by rest and reflection, high tension by relative calm.

As I gazed across the glacier to the peaks beyond I could not help remembering the momentous morning 20 years before when, as a nervous and unathletic schoolboy, I had taken my first hesitant steps on rock. The crag was a scruffy, smoke-blackened gritstone outcrop called Wharncliffe Crags. My first climb: Black Slab, Difficult, 9m (30ft). I have now done thousands of climbs throughout the world, but the details of every move and the sheer excitement of that first climb are burnt on my memory. I knew within minutes that rock climbing was to be the sport for me, not because I showed any unusual aptitude, but just because it struck so resonant a chord. This is not uncommon. Very few people are lukewarm about climbing and those taking it up either give it up very quickly or start a lifelong passion.

I look back on my own early years as a climber with great nostalgia and affection, but also with some horror at the mistakes that we made and risks that we took through ignorance. For instance, I remember the touching faith that we had in the strength of 5mm (⅕in) nylon line and am grateful that its meagre breaking strain was never shown up by a serious fall. I hope that this book will help you to avoid some of the more threatening pitfalls that you will encopunter on the exciting path of your development as a climber.

History

Hunters and travellers in wild country have for thousands of years scaled rocks as part of their journeys, but the emergence of rock climbing as a sport was relatively late. The Victorians were active in the exploration and development of mountaineering in the Alps and many of the great alpine peaks were first ascended by parties in which British mountaineers provided the driving force. These mountaineers began to use the rocks of Snowdonia and the Lake District as training grounds for their alpine excursions, but the traditional birthplace of rock climbing as an independent sport is usually claimed to be the ascent of Napes Needle in 1886 by W. P. Haskett-Smith. This ascent of a detached and exposed pinnacle on the southern flank of Great Gable in the Lake District was, it seems, made through sheer *joie de vivre* and without the encumbrance of ropes or companions. A handkerchief was left on the summit as evidence to those who might follow.

This ascent seemed to trigger a tremendous growth in the number of rock climbs done on British crags. Many of these have remained classic ascents that provide grand climbing where you are literally in touch with the handholds and footholds of the pioneers.

By the time of the First World War some astonishing climbs had been achieved, particularly since equipment and protection systems were extremely rudimentary. A tweed suit, a pair of nailed boots and a length of hemp line constituted the equipment available and the dictum was simple: 'The leader must not fall'.

Some of the finest climbers of the pioneering era died in the First World War, but the tradition continued into the 1920s and 1930s as climbers ventured onto ever steeper rocks and ever smaller holds. Some of the classic climbs of this period by climbers such as Colin Kirkus, J. Menlove Edwards or Jim Birkett still command considerable respect and few of them are climbs for beginners. At the same time climbers experimented with improved rope techniques and the use of karabiners and elementary protection techniques to safeguard the leader against the consequences of a slip.

Security for the leader was still, however, largely illusory and an early attempt on Mickledore Grooves on the East Buttress of Scafell saw the leader slipping from the final holds and falling 50m (165ft) or more almost to the ground.

In parallel with the developments in Britain alpinists elsewhere were turning their attention to crag climbing. By the 1930s high standard crag climbs had been established in many countries and active development was taking place in Eastern Europe, California, Colorado, South Africa and Australia. In the Dolomites, the Julian Alps and the Mont Blanc massif, rock-climbing standards of the highest difficulty were reached on rocky Alpine peaks.

Except for the exploits of remarkable individuals such as Kellett, climbing without companions on Ben Nevis, war again forced a pause on the development of rock climbing. The 1950s were dominated by the two giant figures of Joe Brown and Don Whillans. Practically every major cliff in Britain and a great many minor ones saw climbs of tremendous quality and difficulty from these two talented individuals and Joe Brown's Welsh masterpieces of Cenotaph Corner and Vector are, for many, the definitive 'hard' climbs. Ex-War Department nylon rope, widely available karabiners and the import of specialist French rock-climbing boots (developed for the sandstone boulders of Fontainebleau) supported this leap in standards and greatly improved the safety of the leader.

By the early 1960s a considerable number of climbers were operating at a standard that only ten years before would have been considered impossible. Joe Brown's influence continued and he was closely involved in a new wave of development on the awesome sea cliffs of Anglesey in North Wales. The development of specialist equipment moved apace and protection techniques became sophisticated to the point where leader falls on the hardest climbs were almost routine. Increasingly difficult climbs would be subdued by climbers pulling directly on pieces of protection equipment until there arose a backlash against this overuse of artificial aids. A new ethic of 'pure' unaided climbing began to be widely talked about and, in some cases, implemented. Climbers were being influenced by developments in Australia and the USA, France and Eastern Europe and the use of specific strength training, gymnasts' chalk and improved protection techniques supported another leap in standards. Peter Livesey was the dominant figure in this period and thus the sport continued, fuelled by fierce competition between the leading performers and supported (both literally and metaphorically) by ever more sophisticated equipment. In particular the developments of camming devices that hold in previously unusable cracks and of rock boots soled with the same kind of high-friction rubber that makes Grand Prix racing cars stick to the track have made a tremendous difference both to the average climber and to those at the leading edge of the sport.

Climbing now

Every generation is astonished by the leap in standards that the next generation brings. At the highest level climbing is a sport as demanding and as specialized as any Olympic event, but by savouring the classics of the past the moderate climber or those no longer in the first flush of youth can relive some of the great moments of climbing history.

An enormous number of climbs and crags have been developed. Climbers can choose routes that are anything from 5m (16ft) to 500m (1650ft) in length; they can climb in the solitude of the remote Scottish Highlands or weekend hurly-burly of a popular gritstone outcrop or artificial climbing wall; they can climb on gritstone, granite, sandstone or any of a dozen other rocks and can climb on cliffs that rise out of the sea or ones that fall into an urban quarry. This tremendous variety has been created and is still being created by the sustained exploratory efforts of generations of climbers.

It would be a fascinating climbing education to climb your way through a progression of the milestones of climbing history, but most of us reach a level of difficulty that prevents us progressing very much further. We may develop a strong affinity with the climbs of a particular period, or even those of a particular climber. Just as the music of Mozart can be relied upon to provide apparently effortless elegance, fans of the climbs of the late Don Whillans bandy about words such as 'powerful', 'uncompromising', 'intimidating', which are almost descriptions of the climber himself!

My own formative years in climbing were in the thrall of the routes of Joe Brown in North Wales: The Grooves, Cenotaph Corner, Vember and Red Wall, climbs to savour and enjoy again and again. I first did Cenotaph Corner (figure 1.1) in the mid-1960s when, during our school holidays, three of us lived a troglodyte existence underneath the Cromlech Boulders, huge detached blocks of rock that originated from Dinas Cromlech at some point in its geological past to leave the monstrous corner of Cenotaph. The climb seemed hard and exciting, but things went well and we ran down to our camp euphoric that we had 'arrived' as climbers. The 'Corner' had fallen! I set off to hitchhike the few miles to Nantperis to buy some groceries and was picked up in a small, green van driven by 'The Baron' himself, Joe Brown – a perfect end to a great day.

Is it safe?

The world at large seems to hold the view that anyone taking up rock climbing is completely mad or at very least has a total disregard for

1.1 Climbing Cenotaph Corner by bridging.

normal standards of safety and propriety. The truth is that rock climbing is nowhere near as dangerous as it appears to be. Modern equipment and protection techniques are so well developed that most of the attendant risk is very much in the control of the individual climber.

It is, of course, impossible to eliminate risk totally. A boulder that has remained in place for millions of years might detach itself and fall on top of you, or you might be struck by lightning. Neither of these events are ones over which you have much control — they are 'Acts of God' or described as 'objective danger'. By proper use of climbers' guide-books and the tremendous range of equipment available, an experienced climber can choose a climb that presents just the right degree of difficulty and the right degree of insecurity.

The degree of difficulty and the degree of risk that a climb might offer are very separate matters. Some extremely hard climbs are so well protected that one would have to make a strenuous effort to sustain an injury by falling. By contrast, some easy climbs, particularly classics or those on roadside crags, are polished to such a glassy finish by the passage of hundreds of thousands of hands and feet that they can present to the uninitiated both insecurity and a lack of proper protection.

I will have much more to say about this in the section about guide books and grades, but the point to emphasize is that the experienced climber can control the level of risk to a very high degree. To eliminate all risk and uncertainty of outcome would be to sanitize the sport but climbers in their 50s, conscious of family responsibilities and diminishing strength, might choose only to climb second on the rope or only climb routes that are known to be well protected and not unduly strenuous. The ambitious rock athlete pushing back the frontiers of the sport undertakes a soul-searching lead without protection in the full knowledge that the consequences of a fall would be extremely severe – life at the top is unforgiving!

A key part of this message is that the experienced climber can make the proper decisions. It is the relative novices who can get into difficulties either because their ambition exceeds their capability or because their ropework and protection technique are inadequate. Erudite climbers are fond of quoting Browning: 'Ah that a man's reach should exceed his grasp, or what's a heaven for?' I applaud the sentiment but am of the strong persuasion that climbers need to be guided safely through their first year or two in the sport, after which they can then make their own decisions about their own approach to risk. That is what this book aims to do.

First steps

If you are reading this book as an absolute beginner and want to start to climb, a number of avenues are possible. The traditional and romantic route is to borrow or steal a washing line and proceed to the nearest crag. This, however, is generally not to be recommended, except for the highly adventurous!

Starting to climb with a more experienced friend can be the ideal way to get to grips with rock climbing. However, you are dependent on the judgement and expertise of that individual. Most climbers are sound and sensible in their approach to safety, but some are not.

If you do not know anyone suitable to fulfil this role then you could join a climbing club. Some are extremely good at dealing with beginners, but most tend to be biased towards the more experienced climber. Some clubs are very elitist indeed and the notoriously intimidating Creag Dhu Climbing Club in Scotland is not likely to give you a sympathetic response! The most sensible course is to find a club in your area and telephone its Secretary to sound out what their attitude might be. Another reliable method is to enrol on a course run by a suitably qualified organization or individual. Some of these take place on climbing walls but most would use natural crags in mountain or moorland areas. A skilled instructor will quickly give you the basis of safe ropework and enough grasp of technique for you to be able to take on easier climbs yourself.

Finally, climbing walls now offer you the chance to sample the gymnastic side of the sport and some of its techniques together with a great opportunity to meet other climbers. Do not be too disheartened if the climbing on walls seems difficult — it is usually designed that way to help the training of experienced climbers. Stick with it and you will make rapid progress.

2

Personal equipment

Having the right equipment is half the battle. You can climb 5m (16ft) granite boulders in the California desert or rockfaces on Himalayan peaks at over 7000m (23000 ft) – but you have to match your clothing and equipment to the situation. At one end of the spectrum, you might climb with little more than a pair of shorts and a pair of rock boots. At the other, heavily insulated boots and clothing and specialized harnesses might be the order of the day.

However, rock climbing on alpine peaks and in the greater ranges is best considered as one of the much wider skills of alpine mountaineering. Most active rock climbers do not operate in an alpine environment but on individual crags typically between 10m (33ft) and 150m (500ft) in height. It is at this particular area of the climber's activity that this book is aimed.

Many people have started rock climbing without any specialized personal equipment, simply using a pair of sports shoes and a direct tie onto the rope, but most climbers will quickly want to acquire the absolute essentials – rock boots, harness and preferably a helmet too.

Rock boots

Climbers on traditional routes or those on long alpine-type ascents might use stiff alpine boots with substantially cleated soles, but the vast majority of active rock climbers will use smooth-soled specialist rock boots.

Legs are very much stronger than arms and one of the first lessons to be learnt is that high quality footwork is essential to make the most of your capabilities as a climber. Rock boots (figure 2.1) provide the crucial link between your foot and the rock and allow you to exploit every opportunity for adhesion that exists.

The perfect rock boot would allow you to stand effortlessly on tiny rugosities the size of a match head, adhere by friction alone to steeply sloping rock and bunch the foot into a compact fist-like unit that can be jammed securely into cracks; and the boot would have a slim, pointed toe to allow it to fit into the tiny pockets common in limestone. Of course, the perfect boot does not exist and every design is a compromise between these often conflicting demands. A serious climber operating at

(a)

(b)

(c)

COLEG POWYS - BRECON

2.1 (a) Rock shoe; (b) all-purpose rock boot; (c) rock slipper.

the highest levels will almost certainly have a number of different pairs of boots which can be matched exactly to the expected demands of a particular climb or a particular rock type rather in the way a golfer might select the correct club or a skier the proper flex of ski.

However, except at the very highest levels, it is possible to get very good performance from a single pair of general-purpose rock boots.

Rock boots fit very snugly around the foot and will usually have a smooth but high-friction sole of butyl rubber extending for 2.5–5cm (1–2in) over the upper of the boot in what is called a *rand*. The rand improves the adhesion of the boot when used for foot-jamming in cracks and also, in more gymnastic manoeuvres, allows the heel to be hooked over suitable holds.

Types of boot

The uppers of the boot are usually made from thin suede leather or canvas with laces that extend down close to the toe, although some specialist boots are of slipper construction, rather like a pair of ballet shoes.

Friction boots are soled with soft, high-friction rubber and are deliberately built without excessive stiffness so that they can conform easily to the contours of the rock. This means that they are more difficult to use for 'edging' (using the boot's inner edge) on extremely small holds. In this situation a boot with much more side-to-side stiffness is desirable – an *'edging' boot*.

Most modern boots have a toe which is reasonably pointed. If you expect to climb frequently on limestone crags, particularly those with the deep pockets called *gouttes d'eau* in France, a pointed toe that almost allows the big toe to fit into the hold is desirable.

The best all-round choice for the relative beginner is a general boot with sufficient stiffness to allow reasonably comfortable edging. Until you have developed the strength in your feet, the softness of friction boots may present problems. On the most technical climbs, very low-cut boots are used to provide maximum ankle flex, but I dislike this style for general use because of the exposure of the ankle bones to the rock and, during the descent, to brambles and scree.

The correct fit

Probably the most important aspect of choosing a boot is achieving the correct fit. The best designed boot in the world is useless if your foot slides about loosely inside it. A well-fitting boot, especially the lighter ones used by high standard climbers, gives a tremendous sensitivity to the contours of the rock and the possibilities of a particular hold. Unfortunately, all boots stretch to a greater or lesser degree in use and so it is difficult at the point of purchase to be sure which size to buy.

Having decided the broad characteristics of the boot that I want to buy, I generally try on several different models before choosing the one that seems to match the shape of my foot. I have found that if I buy a boot which is a tight but not quite excruciating fit with bare feet, after a few days' use the boot will have stretched to a point where it is efficient and acceptably comfortable with very thin socks. If you intend to climb at the highest grades you will be willing to endure considerable pain in order to achieve the most efficient fit, but for climbing at more modest levels on longer climbs aim for a boot that you do not have to remove every 30 minutes.

Different models of boot stretch to differing degrees and a good climbing shop will be able to advise you on this. Even better, some of them have small sections of climbing wall where you can actually get the feel of how a new boot might perform. If you are able to do this, then pay particular attention to the inside edge of the boot between the big toe and the ball of the foot. This is the part that gets the greatest use and needs to give you a feeling of confidence in its adhesion to small holds.

I am afraid that anyone who climbs for a number of years will sooner or later buy a pair of boots which they can hardly bear to wear because they are simply too small. I can still remember the pain endured when I bought a new pair of boots for a rock-climbing holiday in California. They performed superbly for a couple of days' use on cold, north-facing crags in the Highlands of Scotland, but in the fierce heat of the Californian summer my feet expanded much more quickly than the boots. I cannot recommend descending boulder gullies in bare feet!

Soles

Although modern boots give a superb performance on clean, dry rock, they can be lethal unless used with great care on the steep vegetation (particularly dry grass) often encountered during descents. This is a very common cause of accidents and it is all too easy after a difficult ascent to relax your concentration during what might appear to be a relatively innocuous descent.

For similar reasons, when starting a climb it is best if the sole of the boot is in a clean condition. Wash any mud off the sole at the end of a day's climbing and, before starting a climb, double-check that the sole is quite literally 'squeaky clean' on its inside edge. Spit and the palm of the hand will do an adequate job, particularly if you avoid standing on damp ground by stepping off a piece of old towel or your empty rucksack. It is crucial to the success of the climb to establish a positive attitude during the first few feet of the route and slipping from the first holds because the sole of your boot is thinly coated in sheep droppings is not an auspicious start.

Caring for boots

When you return from climbing it is worth unpacking your boots and allowing them to dry in a cool, airy place as this undoubtedly extends their life. If the boots have been thoroughly soaked they do tend to shrink and this can sometimes be used to your advantage with a pair of boots that have stretched more than you would wish.

Harnesses

It is perfectly possible to tie directly onto the end of the rope by using a knot such as a bowline with a suitable stopper knot (see Chapter 4 on knots). I took my first fall as a leader whilst tied onto the rope in this way and, save for a few minor bruises and damaged pride, experienced no problems. However, a purpose-made harness that takes the weight of the body on the legs and buttocks is not only more comfortable but can also be of life-saving importance. Quite simply, because of the constriction on the diaphragm, a person suspended free (out of contact with the rock) on a simple waist tie will, if unaided, experience so much pain that within three or four minutes they will be unable to help themselves and,

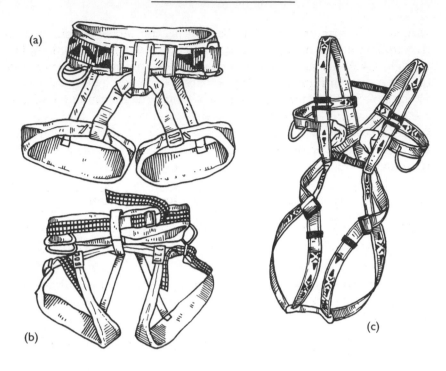

2.2 (a) General-purpose sit-harness (b) with adjustable leg loops. (c) Full-body harness.

shortly afterwards, will lose consciousness and die. It is uncommon for a climber who slips to be totally out of contact with the rock, but it does happen. The investment in a suitable sit-harness or full-body harness (figure 2.2) can make the difference between a life-threatening crisis and a resolvable, albeit considerable, difficulty.

Sit-harnesses

A simple climber's belt made of a length of broad and strong nylon webbing with a secure buckle is an improvement on the simple waist tie direct to the rope, but still presents the same difficulties to a free-hanging climber. I would strongly recommend that you purchase a sit-harness. A wide variety of these are available and whilst almost all will be safe if properly used, it is important to find one that meets your particular requirements. All will be constructed from nylon webbing which may or may not have some degree of padding and decoration. If you expect to confine your activities mainly to crag climbing then a simple harness with a buckled waist belt and attached leg loops is likely to be perfectly adequate. If, however, you might be involved in alpine climbing or winter climbing then some degree of adjustment in the leg loops is desirable, to allow for differences in the bulk of your clothing and also to allow for calls of nature on high mountains.

The link between the rope and your harness is crucial and a simple, foolproof system is essential. It is vital to follow the manufacturer's recommendations in buckling the harness and attaching the climbing rope. Most buckles require 'doubling back' and will not hold a fall if this is omitted.

My own preference is for a harness which:

- Allows a direct tie-in of the rope rather than requires the use of a screwgate karabiner.
- Has a simple and unmistakable buckling system.
- Has a number of equipment loops to allow karabiners and slings to be carried around the waist.
- Has slight padding.
- Is provided with a separate loop built into the system to carry the karabiner for the belay plate.
- Has a loop at the back suitable for holding a chalk bag.

Chapter 4 explains 'belaying' (using a rope for security) and the use of the metal linking devices known as karabiners.

Full-body harnesses

In France and Germany it is common to see climbers using full-body harnesses and it is likely that in a very severe fall such harnesses can give the body better protection against back injury and ensure that the climber is suspended head-up. However, full-body harnesses are generally less convenient in use than the sit-harnesses which are much more common in Britain and North America. I use a sit-harness for rock climbing, mainly because it is a lighter option and because I prefer the attachment point to the rope to be at my waist rather than at chest level. I do wear a full-body harness for alpine ski mountaineering where there is often the possibility of a fall into a hidden glacier crevasse and being suspended, hanging freely from the rope.

The correct fit

When buying a harness it is important to remember that its prime purpose is to divert the impact of a fall from the vulnerable parts of your body to the stronger regions of your thighs, buttocks and back. For this to happen, the harness design needs to match your particular anatomy. We are all different in the relative shapes and sizes of the parts of our bodies and what can be an extremely comfortable harness for one person can be at best uncomfortable and, at worst, possibly dangerous on another person. Some manufacturers have started to recognize this by bringing out not only different sizes of a harness but also different proportions of the component parts in, for example, a women's version. Most specialist retailers of rock-climbing equipment will allow you to suspend yourself while you literally 'hang about' for a few minutes to find the weak spots of the harness (or, indeed, of your body). Men will probably need little persuasion to ensure that load-bearing pieces of webbing do not threaten the more delicate parts of their anatomy.

There is one well-known model of harness that has successfully held people in very considerable falls, but I have always suspected that it was not suitable for everyone. Once, I was climbing with a friend who used this harness, on a climb called Subsidiary Grooves on Cyrn Las, a dark, forbidding cliff in North Wales. He was struggling up a strenuous 'corner' near the top of the climb when he slipped and took a short fall. The fall was held easily, but he complained that he had landed rather uncomfortably in the harness. Within a few minutes he was in great pain and soon after almost delirious. Fortunately we were by that stage at the top of the climb and I was able to get him down to the road and my car and rush him off to hospital. Half an hour after my partner's admission the physician came out to see me. 'You were just in time,' he said. 'It was no problem for us to sort it out, but if you had been half an hour longer in getting him here he would probably have lost it.' I must have looked blank. 'He had a twisted testicle,' said the doctor. Now it may have been purely coincidental that this injury took place after the short fall, but since that day I have paid particular attention to getting a good fit from my own climbing harnesses!

Helmets

Whether expert or beginner, anyone who climbs with Outward Bound has to use a helmet. However, go to any popular weekend climbing area and you will see that though helmets are not uncommon the majority of rock climbers will not be using them. In my view, this is a mistake even though I must admit that on occasions I do not use a helmet myself.

The brain is a particularly vulnerable part of the body and so the protection afforded by a helmet can be valuable both in protection against falling objects and if, in the event of a fall, the head strikes the rock. However, balanced against this are other considerations. For many peo-

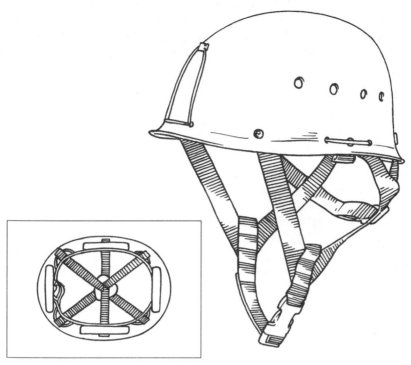

2.3 A good general-purpose climbing helmet. Note the ventilation holes and the internal cradle.

ple, wearing a helmet impedes their sense of balance and there is no doubt that climbers accidentally bang their heads on overhangs much more readily when wearing helmets than not. Also, particularly in hot weather, helmets can be very uncomfortable.

On some crags loose rock is common, particularly in the areas of easy ground at the cliff top. It is very easy for a passing climber or the rope to dislodge stones. By the time these have fallen some distance they are travelling with considerable momentum and can cause serious injury. The main value of a helmet is in reducing the serious consequences of such impacts. Other crags are very well used and have virtually no loose rock. On these, the hazard of loose rock is much smaller although it is always possible that a party climbing above might drop a piece of equipment such as a karabiner, and one can never totally ignore the possibility of rockfall. Most crags are in a state of geological transition and occasionally massive rockfalls can occur in areas previously considered sound.

Obviously, a helmet only provides protection against the small falling stones. I have had three close calls with falling rocks. The first two, in the Himalayas and on Ben Nevis, involved high-speed falling rocks – in one case the size of an armchair, the other of a television set – which crashed down just a few feet from where I was belayed (secured with a rope) to the mountain. In neither case would the helmet have been of the slightest use against a direct impact, but it could have saved my life if I had been unfortunate enough to have been hit by some of the ricocheted fragments. The third near miss was in a much more innocuous situation. We had completed a climb on a limestone outcrop and were sitting on a gentle grass slope at its foot enjoying our lunch when a rock the size of a house brick (and probably dislodged by a careless climber above) thudded into the grass just an arm's length from where I was sitting. This was a very frightening experience, but doubly so because my helmet was sitting use-lessly on the grass beside me. The lesson is clear; if you are going to have lunch at the bottom of a crag, then choose a spot sheltered from stonefall. If you have a helmet and there is any stonefall danger, then do keep it on.

Each individual must make a choice of whether to wear a helmet or not. My own view is that people taking up climbing should wear a helmet at all times, not least because the risks of a falling climber hitting the rock are very much greater on easier-angled climbs. When the climber has more experience and a more informed understanding of the pros and cons, then a proper choice can be made. I always wear a helmet when instructing climbing, to set a good example, and usually wear one for my own climb-ing but I do sometimes make an exception in particularly hot weather. If you are climbing on difficult overhanging rock with good protection you would be unlikely to bash your head in a fall. Most climbers would leave their helmet off in this situation.

Choosing a helmet

Once you decide to buy a helmet, and I hope you will, you then, of course, have a choice. The safest helmets are probably the ones con-structed of glass reinforced plastic (GRP), perhaps with carbon fibres and with a foam lining, but unfortunately they are also the heaviest and the hottest to wear. My preference is for the much lighter and more comfort-able plastic-shelled helmet. I like my helmet to be white in order to min-imize the absorption of heat from the sun, and to have some ventilation holes (figure 2.3).

At least as important as the shell of the helmet is its cradle and harness. An adjustable cradle is useful but the combined cradle and harness must hold the shell securely on the head. When trying on a helmet, subject it to a glancing blow from the front and back. If, as is depressingly com-mon, the helmet rolls off your head then you need to adjust its fitting or use a different helmet. A tumbling fall will subject both the helmet and the climber to very considerable impacts and it requires a very securely attached helmet to withstand this.

Clothing

Fortunately, one can climb in almost any type of clothing that allows reasonable freedom of movement. In Britain, people frequently wear stretchy tracksuit trousers and sweatshirts, whereas in the more intense heat of Australia or North America loose-fitting cotton clothing reflects the heat more successfully.

Increasingly, serious climbers wear the kind of heavyweight lycra tights favoured by athletes. These are a powerful statement that you are a 'hard' climber, but are also thought to increase the degree of kinaesthetic feedback from the limbs and thus improve balance and performance. There is also the view that if you dress in a way that makes you feel athletic and dynamic you are more likely to climb in an athletic and dynamic way. So avoid wearing your gardening clothes for that big lead!

Crags that are well sheltered and face the sun can be exceptionally warm; those that are exposed to the wind or are permanently shadowed can be extremely cold. It is a good idea to have enough flexibility of clothing to deal with these extremes and a lightweight windproof top combined with several thin, insulating layers can be very successful.

Chalk

Athletes' chalk (light magnesium carbonate) started to be used on the hardest climbs in California's Yosemite Valley in the early 1970s. It improves the climber's grip, particularly on smooth, sloping holds, and minimizes the effect of sweaty hands, but you should be aware that there are a number of ethical and environmental considerations relating to the use of chalk (see Chapter 6) and some crags are 'chalk-free zones'. Its use has, however, now spread to all grades except the easiest and most climbers taking up the sport would buy a chalk bag and chalk either in block or powder form (figure 2.4).

Chalk bags

Chalk bags come in various shapes and sizes. Climbers on climbing walls or limestone with small fingerholds might only need a bag large enough to chalk the fingertips, whereas the fierce, hand-jamming cracks of gritstone or granite demand a larger bag so that the hand can be plunged in almost up to the elbow.

The best designs of chalk bag have a wire stiffener to keep the top open, a fleece lining to help the transfer of the chalk to the hand and an

(a)   (b)

2.4 (a) Chalking up on steep rock. (b) Chalk bag

internal sleeve that can be easily tightened to seal the bag. This is useful in preventing chalk escaping whilst the climber is sitting on *stances* or scrambling down easy ground.

Odds and ends

If you only climb on roadside crags, you can probably carry your equipment in a supermarket carrier bag, but if there is any walking involved, a smallish (30–40 litres (7–9 gal)) rucksack is useful. The design is unimportant except that those with an integral foam backpad prevent some of the sharper pieces of climbing equipment digging into your back. You will not want to walk to the crag in your expensive and uncomfortable rock boots, so a pair of training shoes or light hiking boots would be more suitable.

Now to the crag!

3

Moving on rock

Our distant ancestors were climbers long before they mastered the bow and arrow or the stone axe. To learn to rock climb you have to clear away some of the veneer of civilization that tells you what you can and cannot do and discover some of your hidden capabilities. Some of the satisfaction of climbing undoubtedly lies in the fact that it puts us in contact with our own distant origins, something that farmers, hunters and sailors might well recognize.

Unfortunately, for many people their first few hours of climbing are reduced to '15 things you can do with a screwgate karabiner' or the recitation of a litany of climbing calls. Safe ropework and proper communication are very important aspects of safe climbing and this book will pay a great deal of attention to them, but to expect the apprehensive beginner to master more than the very barest minimum is to put the cart before the horse and to stand in the way of the development of actual climbing skills. For this reason, if you can find a suitable place, I strongly recommend that you start climbing with at least a couple of hours of bouldering.

Bouldering

Musicians of all standards will practise the playing of scales to develop fluency, confidence, flexibility and stamina without the distractions of an audience. Bouldering (figure 3.1) – climbing without ropes and close to the ground – is used in the same way by climbers to develop exactly the same qualities. Just as well-practised musicians can be confident that during the big performance their fingers will respond correctly to the complexity of the piece, so the climber on a big climb can climb much more confidently if the basic moves have already been extensively practised near the ground.

The ideal spot for bouldering is an outcrop of rock between 3 and 6m (10 and 20ft) in height with a good 'landing' beneath the rocks so that the climber can jump from difficult problems without undue fear of injury. Flat grass or sand gives a very good landing, whereas some otherwise superb bouldering areas are ruined by being situated above ankle-breaking boulder fields. Sometimes you will find collections of actual boulders in a field with each boulder offering a variety of routes of ascent

3.1 Bouldering.

– some steep, some smooth, some hard, some easy. Often people use the first few feet of a much larger crag for practice purposes. Once, during a family holiday in Portugal, I discovered some superb sea cliffs, nowhere higher than 5m (16ft), often overhanging but with excellent holds and a magnificent landing in soft sand. In desperation, urban climbers will boulder on buildings. This 'buildering' is a poor substitute for the real thing and (not surprisingly) is most unpopular with janitors.

Let us assume that you have found a suitable boulder – one which is not too steep, on which even the uninitiated can spot some holds and with the all-important good landing. Put on your boots and helmet and, ensuring that your feet are clean and dry, step onto the rock to get the feel of this unfamiliar medium.

Traversing

The best way to stay close to the ground is by traversing – moving crab-wise across the piece of rock whilst staying within a metre or so of the ground. You will rapidly discover that your rock boots have remarkable powers of adhesion if you use them properly. Generally speaking, they will work much more effectively if you stand out from the rock with your centre of gravity over your feet. If you lean in, on sloping footholds your weight will start to push the boot from the hold; this means that you cannot stretch too far for holds. Indeed, you will probably have to reappraise what you consider to be a hold anyway. If you are on rocks up to about 65 degrees of angle (a climber would call this a 'slab') then you can, with the right footholds, support all or most of your weight on your feet and need only small fingerholds to aid your balance.

In traversing the boulder you will also discover that rock climbing is a problem-solving exercise, and just as a chess player has to be creative in the deployment of the pieces, so a climber must experiment with different sequences of holds, or holds used in different ways. One of the charms of rock climbing is that the solution of a particular piece of rock depends on a variety of factors including the build of the climber, so what works for your companion might not work for you and vice versa. Some of the greatest climbers have possessed tremendous 'rock intelligence' – an ability to look at a difficult piece of rock and immediately know what techniques to apply and what sequence of holds to use. Others find that they must succeed by dogged persistence and the elimination of every unsuccessful alternative.

Holds

So, as you climb, concentrate on what the movement feels like and develop an awareness of your hands and feet on the holds. This awareness will quickly make you appreciate some of the fundamentals such as keeping the hands low on problems near the limit of foot friction or keeping the foot still once it is correctly placed on a small hold.

When you have crossed your boulder, do not step down at the far end but reverse your steps. You may be reversing the same route but you will probably find that you need an entirely different sequence of moves. If this goes smoothly, repeat your original route but this time try to eliminate one or two of the larger holds, climbing past without their use. Next, you can try to do the same traverse by only using one hand. This is particularly good for developing a good sense of balance since the body must be carefully poised before the one permitted hand is moved from one hold to the next.

Experiment with smaller and smaller footholds (figure 3.2) until you understand the limits of adhesion of your boot and explore the variety of different handholds that you can use. Simple fingerholds are obvious, but less so is the fact that side pulls – vertical edges or sideways flakes of rock – can provide tremendous assistance to your balance and progress. Even 'upside down' holds such as downward-pointing spikes are of great value

3.2 (a) Using a small foothold. (b) Climbing a slab. (c) Using a side pull for the right hand. (d) Fingers 'crimped' on a small hold.

if you pull upwards on them against the pressure of your feet. Then move on to a different boulder, perhaps something steeper and continue to explore the possibilities.

Most newcomers to rock climbing neglect the use of their feet and over-emphasize the use of handholds. This tendency is reinforced by the

natural instinct to hang on to the rock for dear life! When you are bouldering, try to overcome this tendency and place as much emphasis as you
possibly can on standing on your feet in a balanced, athletic stance.

Safety and fitness

If you choose the right place bouldering is safe, but you can reduce the
risks by staying close to the ground and, if things become too difficult,
jumping off rather than waiting for a fall to occur. Finally, it is much
safer to climb with companions and you can then 'spot' each other, with
one person climbing and the other ready to give support in the event of a
slip and to break any awkward fall.

Bouldering is a brilliant way to start climbing and it is also a tremendously important means of keeping your mind and body in trim throughout your climbing career. Some climbers, notably John Gill in the USA,
have developed bouldering to such a level of athletic virtuosity and Zen-
like concentration that they rarely involve themselves in conventional
roped climbing. However, the great majority of climbers are thoroughly
glad of the protection given by the rope, which enables them to climb
very much further from the ground than the principles of bouldering
can allow.

Protection by the rope

The rope provides the metaphorical safety net above which the climber
performs. With its proper use and that of the equipment associated with
it, the consequences of a slip are usually trivial for the second person on
the rope and very much reduced for the first. Contrary to popular belief,
climbers do not ascend ropes hand over hand and the rope is only used to
provide direct assistance to progress on rare and specialized occasions.
Modern techniques of using the rope and other protection equipment are
now so well developed that on the hardest climbs falls of even 10–15m
(33–50ft) can often be sustained without serious consequences.

The idea behind the use of the rope is simple. It links members of the
party together and only one person moves at any one time. As that person climbs, their rope is managed by another member of the party who,
in the event of a slip, will hold a fall. For this system to work the rope
must be strong and firmly attached to each climber, and the person
controlling the rope (the *belayer*) – must be securely anchored to the
mountainside. Ropes are indeed extremely strong, with a static breaking
load in excess of 2 tonnes, and much of the high-tech protection equipment that is available to climbers exists in order to make it possible to
arrange anchors for the belayer that match or exceed the strength of the
rope.

Belaying and karabiners – some definitions:

- The verb *to belay* means, literally, to make fast. In rock climbing it means to protect a climber with the aid of a rope secured directly or indirectly to an anchor. A climber progressing up a pitch is belayed by a companion who in turn is belayed to a rock feature that provides a secure anchor.
- An *anchor* is any natural rock feature or device lodged in the rock to which a rope can be attached, usually via a karabiner.
- The *belayer* is the person who holds a climber's rope in such a way that a fall can be arrested.
- A *running belay* or *runner* is an intermediate anchor used between the climber and the belayer to reduce the length of a potential fall.
- A *karabiner* is a strong metal linking device used in the belay system. It has a springloaded gate on one side.
- A *screwgate* karabiner has a gate that can be locked in the closed position for extra security.
- A *snaplink* karabiner has no such locking device.

Single-pitch climbs

Most climbing ropes are between 45 and 55m (145 and 180ft) in length and climbs are usually divided into *pitches* – convenient sections of the climb which are less than a complete rope length in extent. Single-pitch climbs (figure 3.3) are a special category. These are climbs, typically 10–40m (33–130ft) in length, on which the belaying (rope-holding) climber can sit at the top of the climb securing the rope of the climber as the latter leaves the ground and ascends the rocks ahead. When the climbers are united at the top of the crag, they can then descend, usually by walking down an 'easy way'.

Multi-pitch climbs

Multi-pitch climbs (figure 3.4) are typically of 30–300m (100–980 ft). Here the first climber will ascend the first pitch of the climb, a distance of less than a single rope length, anchor themselves to the mountain and then protect (belay) the second climber ascending to the stance from where the belay is being taken. One of the climbers will then move upwards on the second pitch of the climb, find a stance and anchor and then repeat the process. For experienced parties, the rope of two is most common and the system is at its most efficient when the climbers leapfrog by leading alternate pitches. You will probably see by this stage

3.3 A single-pitch climb. (a) The leader climbs the pitch, belayed by the second, who is anchored to the rock. This is often omitted if there is no danger of a slip by the second, or if the second is heavy enough to provide an efficient counterbalance to the weight of a falling leader on a runner. (b) The leader has placed a runner. (c) The second climbs, protected by the leader who is now anchored.

that once the system has been established for the ascent of two consecutive pitches it can then be used for any subsequent number. This is the basic system of security by which climbs of even several hundred metres in length are ascended.

It is easy to see how the second or subsequent person on the rope can be protected during their ascent by the rope which extends above them.

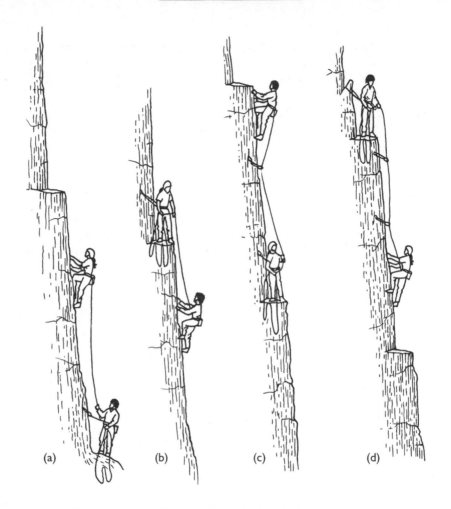

(a)   (b)   (c)   (d)

3.4 A multi-pitch climb. (a) The first climber leads and (b) reaches a stance, securing themselves and belaying the second. (c) The second climbs past and leads the next pitch. Here a runner is shown. (d) A second stance is reached and the process is repeated.

What is less apparent is how the first climber – the *leader* – is also able to attain some security. When climbing technology was less well developed, leaders had to be of a courage and a competence such that they simply would not fall. These days, although leading is a much more serious affair than seconding, the leader does have some leeway and with skill can usually attain a good level of security by the use of 'runners' or running belays.

Runners

While climbing, the leader will attach intermediate anchors to the rock which are connected to the rope with a karabiner or snaplink. A long pitch may well involve the use of 15 or more such runners (figure 3.5). As the leader extends the rope up the pitch, it is secured by the second climber. If the leader should slip, as long as the anchor of the runner is secure, the length of the fall is greatly reduced.

Top roping

Because leading is considerably more intimidating than seconding, single-pitch climbers will sometimes operate in a way that renders it unnecessary for anyone to lead the pitch. This is by a technique known as *top roping* and there are two main systems.

The first is very like conventional pitching but instead of leading to the top of the cliff the first climber will ascend by a path or easy route, find an anchor and then drop the end of the rope down the climb to the second, who can then ascend when belayed.

If the height of the crag is less than half of one rope length, then a related technique called *bottom roping* can be used (figure 3.6). Here the rope runs from the belayer, standing at the foot of the cliff, through a karabiner attached to the anchor at the top of the cliff and then back down to the moving climber. This system can only be conveniently applied to climbs of less than one rope length in height but it does have the advantage that the movements of the climber are very evident to the belayer. We found bottom roping to be an ideal method for climbing as a family with two children under 5 in tow — always an adult on the ground.

In Chapter 4 we shall look much more closely at how to choose and use a climbing rope and how to use the great variety of available equipment in order to arrange secure anchors for the belaying climber and running belays for the leader. It is now time to look more closely at the rocks on which the climber's sport takes place.

The crag

Stand beneath any extensive crag, especially when evening light picks out its texture, and you will see a great variety of features. You will quickly learn to pick out promising lines of ascent and those to avoid, but first you need to get to grips with the basic terminology.

Slabs and walls

Imagine up-ending a piece of concrete roadway to give a more or less smooth face devoid of other major features. If the angle to the horizontal

3.5 (a) Climber on very steep rock protected by a single rope clipped into a runner. Running a rope: (b) the right way and (c) the wrong way.

(a)

(b)

(c)

3.6 Bottom roping.

to which you have tipped it is between about 40 and about 75 degrees, then you have a *slab*. Crank the angle further and you have a *wall*, which is about 75 degrees or steeper. Once the angle of the wall is past the vertical so that its top overhangs its base, it is often described as an *overhanging wall* (figure 3.7).

Slab climbs (figure 3.2) usually make few demands on the arm strength of the climber, but they require good balance and an imaginative use of often sparse holds. Climbs such as the Outside Edge route on Craig Cwm Silyn in Snowdonia or the Grande Miroir d'Argentine in Switzerland provide exhilarating outings at a reasonable standard because they are huge slabs well equipped with small and positive holds. The climber is in a genuine 'fly-on-the-wall' situation but, because strength is not at a premium, is in a position to savour the situation.

Harder slab climbs can be very scary indeed and often require great boldness and an extremely positive attitude if the climber is to succeed. The climbs of the Glacier Point Apron in Yosemite or the Etive Slabs in Western Scotland are inspiring examples of this. The Apron requires the climber to use the tiniest fingernail-size rock flakes and rock crystals to cross intimidatingly smooth, glacier-polished sweeps of granite. If the Etive Slabs were a few degrees less steep they would probably have sheep wandering across them but, as it is, the climbing is often by pure friction and very close to the angle at which the adhesion between boot and rock entirely ceases.

On walls the climber must have handholds to sustain balance and this begins to make greater physical demands on fingers and arms. Fortunately, some vertical and overhanging walls do seem to have more than their fair share of large holds (figure 3.7). These are known as *jugs* (from 'jug handles') in the UK, whilst across the Atlantic climbers are more inclined to talk about *buckets*. Whatever you call them, such holds are extremely welcome, as are *spikes* (UK) or *chicken heads* (USA), both of which are substantial protruding mini-pinnacles of rock that can be grasped with enthusiasm.

A slab at such an easy angle that you can walk easily across it, is called a *glacis*. At the other end of the scale, when an overhanging wall approaches the horizontal, it is then called a *roof* or *ceiling*. Such features are always strenuous!

3.7 (a) A 'jug'. (b) An overhanging wall – it is best to climb quickly here!

Terminology does vary from region to region. At the risk of confusing you completely, I should perhaps point out that American climbers often call a very large crag a 'wall' and describe what their British counterparts call 'wall climbing' as 'face climbing'. Fortunately, most climbing guide books adopt a uniform style and may even have a glossary of particularly local terms.

Grooves and corners

When two walls come together to form an angle of approximately 90 degrees like the inside corner of a room this is called a *corner* or, in the USA, a *dihedral* (or in France a *dièdre*, which means the same thing). When walls meet at a more obtuse or acute angle than 90 degrees the resultant feature is called a *groove*, which can be deep or shallow, over-hanging or easy-angled and so on. More often than not, corners and grooves have a crack in their angle and often provide the lines which climbs follow. One of the most famous rock climbs in the world, the Nose of El Capitan in California, is over 920m (3000ft) high and for much of its height follows connecting systems of grooves and corners.

Grooves and corners are the great architectural features of crags and it is exhilarating to climb them. The two sidewalls often allow you to use a technique called *bridging* or *stemming* where, by straddling the groove with your feet, you can get more into balance by moving your centre of gravity inside your points of support on each wall. This means that it is sometimes possible to get a hands-off rest even when the groove overhangs.

Cracks and chimneys

In the distant days when, newly made, the crag cooled from a semi-molten state or when, much later, it was subjected to the thrusts and cat-aclysmic forces of mountain building, cracks and fissures developed through the rock.

Sometimes these are tiny hairline faults extending for a few centi-metres, sometimes major fault-lines tens of metres wide and hundreds of metres in length. Fissures up to about 30cm (12in) in width are called *cracks*. When they are between 30cm (12in) and about 150cm (5ft) they are called *chimneys* (figure 3.8). When wider than this they would usu-ally be called *gullies* or *couloirs*. You do not need to take your measuring stick on the climb because what determines the nomenclature is whether or not the climber can fit inside. If a climber has to climb on the outside of the fissure it will usually be called a crack. If the climber can climb within the feature, it has become a chimney. If the walls of the fissure are too wide for the climber to straddle or to back-and-foot (using opposing

(a)   (b)

3.8 (a) A chimney climbed by back-and-knee, a knee bar and low hand pressure. (b) A steep handcrack climbed with hand jams but with helpful footholds on the wall.

pressure with the back against one wall and the feet against the other) then you are probably in a gully system.

I have already told you that climbing is a very natural activity and so it is – if you are climbing on positive holds. However, what makes crack climbing so interesting is that to be successful you must master the proper techniques.

Finger cracks

In finger cracks, which are typically 2–3 cm (¾–1in) in width, the fingers can be placed in a crack just above a constriction. Particularly if the hand is placed thumb-down, the effect of the constriction and the torque (twist) on the fingers gives a very secure hold (figure 3.9). The feet can either use small holds beside the crack, if these exist, or the toe of the boot can be jammed into the crack. Again, this is often most secure if a degree of torque can be applied by angling the ankle and pivoting the knee sideways. As finger cracks are ideally sized for the placement of nuts (metal wedges) and small camming devices (see Chapter 4), they tend to offer climbing that is both intricate and well protected.

Hand cracks

Hand cracks (figure 3.8) are wider – 5–20cm (2–8 in) and here the *hand jam* (figure 3.9) is ubiquitous. A well-placed hand jam is every bit as secure as the most positive handhold, with the added advantage that less energy is required to maintain it. For the ideal hand jam, select a local widening of the crack into which your hand will slide easily and then expand your hand by angling it at the knuckles or moving the thumb across to expand the heel of the hand and the base of the thumb. When the hand fits imperfectly in the crack, either because it is too wide or narrow or because the crack is flared, then more force has to be applied to make the hand jam hold. The use of chalk will often make poor jams of this kind feel somewhat more secure. The toe of the boot can be jammed as for finger cracks but foot placements tend to be more secure (if no less painful). Very good protection can be obtained from large camming devices.

Fist cracks

Fist cracks tend to be 10–15cm (4–6in) in width. I have never mastered the art of fist jamming (figure 3.9) without pain though others assure me that it is possible. The clenched fist is placed sideways or crossways above a narrowing in the crack and pressure is applied. *In extremis*, both fists can be 'stacked' and placed side by side. The feet can either be torqued in fist cracks or jammed crossways with the heel on one wall and the toe on the other.

Off-widths

Off-widths are the *bête noire* of most climbers. They are too wide to be climbed as hand or fist cracks but too narrow to be climbed as chimneys. Climbing in them is almost always strenuous and almost always intimidating because it is usually insecure and often badly protected. Californian granite and Derbyshire gritstone are both notorious for some of their off-widths. The description of Right Eliminate at Curbar Edge in the British Mountaineering Council guide book captures the essence:

> The energy expended on each ascent could light Sheffield for a week. Follow the wide crack making 2 moves up and one down until the ordeal is over. Strangely tempting.

Off-width techniques can be esoteric. Once you are in the crack it is very difficult to see what hands and feet are doing and it is worth working out a strategy first. If there are any holds on the edge of the crack, then face towards them. You will generally climb with one arm and shoulder deep inside the crack, the other near the surface. The inside arm can be very useful if locked by pointing the fingers downwards and pressing the palm against one wall of the crack, the elbow against the other. This unlikely camming movement can give astonishingly good support and is called an *arm-bar*. The other hand is generally reduced to grasping the outside edge of the crack or palming behind you. Feet are jammed in whatever way seems possible. The trick is to exert only enough force to hold yourself in place in the crack and to release this when you wish to move upwards. This is very easy to say and very much more difficult to do!

On easier climbs it is unusual to find more than one or two off-width moves, but some of the harder climbs on the granite of California or Chamonix can have offwidths that extend for 30m (100ft) or more. These give notoriously difficult pitches. On a long pitch of this kind, it is vitally important to face the correct way. Trying to turn around half-way up a long off-width is not recommended.

Chimneys

Many people do not care for chimneys. I can understand this but, after the horrors of the off-width, it is at least a relief to be able to hide inside the depths of a chimney. Chimneys tend to exist on major geological fault-lines and so will often provide a line that extends from the base to the top of the cliff. Many of the climbs done by the pioneers at the end of the nineteenth century followed chimney lines, a period of the evolution of the sport that preceded climbers' moving out onto the more exposed and intimidating open faces.

If a chimney has holds on both faces then it is most easily climbed by bridging with one foot on each wall. If holds are few, the techniques of back-and-knee or back-and-foot must be used. With each of these techniques it is relatively straightforward to hold the body wedged across the chimney but much more difficult to release the pressure between back-and-knee or back-and-foot in order to move upwards. Occasionally, and usually when *in extremis* in very wide chimneys, opposing pressure between shoulder and foot may have to be used for a short distance.

Make a conscious effort to be systematic when climbing chimneys. It is worth facing towards the wall that appears to offer the most footholds and make use of any opportunities for resting that appear. It is usually best to keep the hands low, generally to push on the wall behind you. Handholds appearing above you are often tempting, but in stretching for

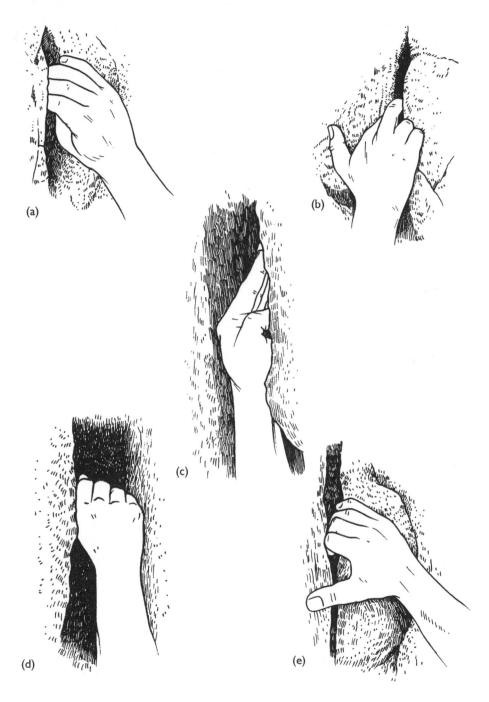

3.9 Handholds in cracks: (a) finger jam; (b) fingerlock; (c) hand jam; (d) fist jam; (e) sprag.

such holds you can be forced to abandon the support that being wedged in the chimney has given you, so this is often a particularly strenuous way of climbing.

Chimneys often have their share of loose rock, sometimes in the form of *chockstones* – large boulders or blocks of rock wedged within the confines of the chimney. Sometimes these are very welcome because they allow the harassed climber to thread them with a long sling (see page 73) and thus arrange some protection, but often they are an inconvenient obstacle that can give the crucial difficulties of a chimney pitch. Sometimes the feasible route of ascent leads deep into the dark recesses of a chimney and becomes much more akin to caving than to climbing.

Finally, chimneys are often dank places with luxuriant alpine vegetation. Whilst this is not to everyone's taste, it does mean that chimneys can be less badly affected by wet weather than most types of climbing but they can also turn into waterfalls during heavy rain.

Flake cracks

When a thin sheet of rock is partly detached from the face beneath it, it is called a flake and the resultant cracks around it are called *flake cracks*. Depending on the width of the crack, any of the techniques already mentioned can be employed but the classic method is to use *laybacking*. This employs the opposing forces generated by pulling hard with the hands on the edge of the crack and pushing very hard with the feet on the wall beside it.

Laybacking (figure 3.10) is a bold and exhilarating way of climbing but it also tends to be strenuous and it can be very difficult to take a hand off to place protection. It is often possible to employ jamming as an alternative or to use a combination of several techniques. When the flake crack faces downwards, or if the crack beneath is an overhang, opposing pressure techniques can still be used and this is often called an *undercling*.

Laybacking is a versatile technique and can in fact be used on many cracks. Off-widths can sometimes be climbed by placing the feet on one edge and laybacking on the other, or a face climb where most of the climbs are side pulls will sometimes yield most readily to the application of layback technique. Laybacking an arête is one of the wildest of all climbing moves.

Rock types

Crags vary tremendously in shape, colour and texture and the biggest influence on this is the type of rock from which they are formed. If you know what kind of rock a crag is made of you can make a pretty good guess as to the style of climbing that it will offer.

Limestone

Limestone cliffs are usually steep and with vertical or overhanging climbing on small but positive holds and pockets. The climbing is impressive but can be less subtle than that on other rock types. Above all, you will need strong fingers.

There is usually a certain amount of loose rock on limestone cliffs and, if the climbs are well frequented, the holds quickly polish to a disconcerting glaze.

Granite

Sometimes granite gives the huge monolithic features that are evident in pictures of the Chamonix Aiguilles or El Capitan in Yosemite, but more typically the rock is slightly off the vertical and presents a tremendous variety of holds from tiny crystals to huge flakes. Within the limits of a single pitch you can be confronted with fiercely strenuous and impossibly delicate balance climbing. For me, granite climbing has everything.

Gritstone

However, many would disagree and in Britain one rock with many *aficionados* is gritstone. Small outcrops of rough-textured gritstone that in earlier times was used to make millstones for grinding corn now offer some of the most technically demanding climbs in the world. The hand jam and friction footholds are the order of the day and if you are new to gritstone it is as well to start a couple of grades below your normal standard.

Volcanic rock

Volcanic rocks tend to give sharper and more positive holds than gritstone and rock such as rhyolite or andesite can give some of the best wall climbs, lines of holds allowing a route up walls that seem impregnably steep.

Sandstone

At its best sandstone can be a superb rock to climb on, rather like the best quality gritstone but more massive and more solid; at its worst it is dangerously loose and crumbly. Sometimes, soft sandstone outcrops are all that are available in a particular area to the rock-starved climber and such rock resources have to be treated with great care. Perhaps the most exciting sandstone in the world is to be found on the fantastic towers of the sandstone of the Czech Republic and eastern Germany. Towers up to 100m (330ft) in height are climbed and there is usually no easy way! The summit of each tower has a metal box in which you can write your name and read the comments of those that have gone before you before descending by abseil.

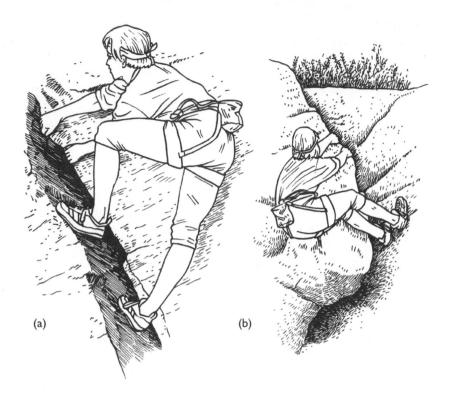

(a)   (b)

3.10 Laybacks: (a) in a corner groove with a wide crack and (b) on an overhanging flake crack. The climber has just got his hands on the helpful upper edge of the flake.

Basalt

Its steep columnar structure makes basalt unmistakable. I have only climbed it on one occasion: the cliff I visited was called Hell's Gate, part of the Great Rift Valley in East Africa. It was about 200m (660ft) in height and tremendously steep. The cracks were among the smoothest that I have ever climbed, with very glassy rock presenting next to no friction – I am unsure whether this was an intrinsic property of the rock or whether it had resulted from polishing by generations of passing baboons and other animals. The atmosphere at Hell's Gate was fiercely impressive! Not only is the crag steep and intimidating, but on the approach you pass the skeletons of baboons who were over-ambitious in their own climbing. At the ledge at the top of a steep and difficult pitch you may well find a snake coiled in wait, whilst all the time the resident lammergeier, a huge East African vulture, circles at the clifftop.

Slate, chalk and pudding stone

There was a time when slate was considered entirely unsuitable for climbing, but in Snowdonia the development of huge faces left by slate quarrying has led to some phenomenally impressive recent climbs. However, I think that it is unlikely that some of the climbs determinedly pioneered on chalk and conglomerate (pudding stone) will ever become popular.

Locations

The nature of a climb also depends on where the crag is situated. The rocks high on Everest are made of limestone (from the shells of marine animals) but the high mountain environment and constant weathering by frost have produced crags very different from, for instance, the limestone sea cliffs of the Pembrokeshire coast. Some of the very finest cliffs are situated in high mountain areas but, since all large mountains breed their own weather, there may be only a few days each year when the weather and the conditions are suitable for an ascent. I once spent three separate weeks in the Charles Inglis-Clark hut on Ben Nevis with the intention of guiding people on some of the best rock climbs in Scotland. During that time I was only able to climb on dry rock for one and a half days. The rest of the time it was either raining or the lichen-encrusted rocks had stayed so damp that they had all the frictional properties of wet liver. However, I am willing to accept that Scotland may well be an extreme case!

Sea cliffs have become highly developed in Britain, particularly on the quartzite of Anglesey and a variety of rocks around the coastline of Devon and Cornwall. Similar climbs have been developed in Brittany and on the tremendous limestone sea cliffs in France and southern Spain.

Some notable climbing areas are found in river gorges, perhaps the most famous examples being the awesome Gorge du Verdon in southern France and parts of the Grand Canyon in Arizona. Climbs on sea cliffs and in deep gorges often have to be approached from above by abseil and this provides a considerable incentive to make a successful ascent once you have pulled down your abseil ropes.

The most popular areas for climbing will offer a variety of different crags – some small, some big, some with easy climbs, some fiercely intimidating, some near the road, some remote. The best approach to finding your way around them is to get hold of a guide book.

Guide books

Guide books may seem an unlikely art form. The true creative act in climbing is the creation of a new route, but the best guide books amplify and give a context to the climb for parties that follow, in much the same way that the best musical or literary criticism adds to a great work of art. At one level, guide books are very much more prosaic and certainly in your early climbing days the important thing is to find the route and to have an understanding of its standard. However, most climbers develop an interest in the history and growth of the sport and in its pioneering personalities.

When climbers make the first ascent of a climb they normally record a description, indicate its provisional grade and choose a name for the climb. Some first ascents will be the result of months of careful training and planning, so the first ascendants put a great deal of effort into coming up with a suitable name. Names can be descriptive, such as Black Slab or Overhanging Wall; they can refer to the pioneers (Kelly's Overhang, Helfenstein's Struggle) or to the effect of the climb on the climber (The Rasp, Kneewrecker Chimney). They might allude to the intimidating power of the climb (Il Duce, Carnivore) or be inspirational (The Ascent of Man, A Dream of White Horses – a climb poised above the breaking sea). Some names are puns, such as Kipling Groove (ruddy 'ard) and Peels of Laughter (to peel is to fall off); other are literary, (Gormenghast, Darkinbad) or musical (Valkyrie, Visions of Johanna) – or virtually anything you like! Some of my particular favourites are Farewell to Arms (a very strenuous climb), Crack of Doom and Vector (a physical quantity with both magnitude and direction).

The writer of the guide book collects all the climbs for a particular area together, checks out the descriptions and endeavours to achieve some consistency in the grading of these climbs before publishing them. The book will usually contain details of access, maps and diagrams or photographs of the crag with route lines marked. On larger crags it is worth taking some time to look at this diagram before you get too close to the crag, when foreshortening can make it difficult to work out what goes where. Here are examples of two descriptions, one for a single pitch hard climb at Stanage (a gritstone edge in Derbyshire) and the other for a classic climb in the English Lake District. Each has the accolade of three stars, thereby denoting climbs of the highest quality.

★★★ **360 Ulysses** 20m [65ft] E6 6b (1983)

The rounded arête right of Goliath's Groove achieved classic status even before it was finally led! An audacious route requiring 'clean' technique and a great deal of psyche. A route for those who would rather be sorry than safe!

(British Mountaineering Council, 1989)

What this climb lacks in height, it makes up for in impact. Finding the climb is straightforward using the clear diagram. Climbing it will not be. The climb is number 360 for Stanage Edge, a very extensive crag, and it is 20m (65ft) in height. The grade is E6 6b, which is pretty fierce (see the section on Grades on page 46) and 1983 is when it was first ascended. At the back of the British Mountaineering Council's 1989 guide is more information on first ascents and you can find out who first did the climb and various snippets of historical background. If you are climbing at this standard it will be clear to you that this is a climb on which you either climb well and successfully or you get hurt – the protection is poor.

★★★ Tophet Wall 75m [245ft] HS 1923

A true classic, winding its way through some very impressive rock architecture. It is one of the best climbs of its grade in the Lake District. Start right of an overhanging crack in the centre of the wall.

1.   20m [65ft]. Climb the wall just right of the crack, until a step left can be made into the crack, which is followed to a ledge. An ascending traverse right leads to a ledge at the foot of the wall. (The original route joins the climb at this point along easy grass ledges from the right.)

2.   17m [55ft]. The wall above is climbed to a broken ledge and corner on the left. Climb the crack in the corner followed by the right wall, to a slab that leads to a corner.

3.   15m [50ft]. Semi-hand traverse 10 metres [33ft] right in a sensational position, to a corner. Climb the rib on the right to a ledge.

4.   23m [75ft]. Ascend the small pinnacle on the right, then step left into the crack which is followed to a rock ledge. Easy climbing leads to the top of the ridge.

(Fell and Rock Climbing Club, 1988)

This climb is about one hour's walk from the road and one needs first to find the cliff! A clear diagram helps you to find the start of this middle-grade classic. Athletic beginners are quite likely to do a 'Hard Severe' very early in their climbing career, perhaps even on their first day, but the traverse on Pitch 3 of the climb may not be well protected for the second climber.

A great asset to the international climber is the increasing use of 'topos' or topographical diagrams which show the line of the climb with a minimum of narrative description (figure 3.11).

Grades

Many of the difficulties that you might encounter when climbing are sub-jective so no grading system can be precise. Different areas have developed different grading systems and they all seem to work well if you use one particular system regularly and become familiar with its quirks.

Perhaps the most logical system is the Australian one, which is entirely open-ended and which starts from 1 and uses increasing numbers for increasing difficulty, so that a Grade 17 is a little harder than a Grade 16 and an awful lot easier than a Grade 23, and so on. The British system combines an adjectival grade for the overall difficulty with a so-called technical grade for harder climbs. Thus, Tophet Wall, Hard Severe, would be regarded as a middle-grade climb, for the sequence of grades is as fol-lows: Easy, Moderate, Difficult, Very Difficult, Severe, Hard Severe, Very Severe, Hard Very Severe, Extremely Severe. Most beginners would quickly manage a climb of Very Difficult standard in good conditions, but climbs of Severe and harder begin to make greater demands on technique.

When this adjectival system was developed, Extremely Severe climbs were the preserve of a very small number of the best climbers. Standards of performance have escalated so much that climbing Extremely Severe climbs is almost commonplace and the grade has had to be made open-ended by using E1, E2, E3, and so on. We are currently at E9 or E10, but watch this space!

On the harder climbs, a technical grade is used and you can only get to know this through familiarity and by comparison. Technical grades ascend as follows: 4a, 4b, 4c, 5a, 5b, 5c, 6a, 6b, 6c, and so on. Roughly speaking, Very Severe climbs will be 4b, 4c or 5a; Hard Very Severe will be 4c, 5a or 5b; E1 will be 5a, 5b, 5c, and so on. The degree of overlap is related to the degree of protection, thus a climb graded VS 5a will be technically difficult but well protected and 'safe' whereas a climb that is graded E1 5a will be of a similar technical difficulty but will be a much more serious undertaking, possibly with loose rock and poor protection in an intimidating situation. The combination of the grade and the guide-book description helps the climber to avoid some of the most unsuitable climbs, but the system, of course, is not foolproof.

In the USA different levels of scrambling or unroped climbing are graded. Roped climbing is called 'fifth class' and the grades are 5.1, 5.2, 5.3, etc. A grade of 5.7 would be roughly equivalent to British VS 4c and 5.9 to E1 5b. The upper grades are subdivided (just as are British E grades) into 5.10a, 5.10b, 5.10c, and so on. Alpine grades run from I–VI with further subdivisions marked by a plus or minus symbol or (a), (b), (c), etc.

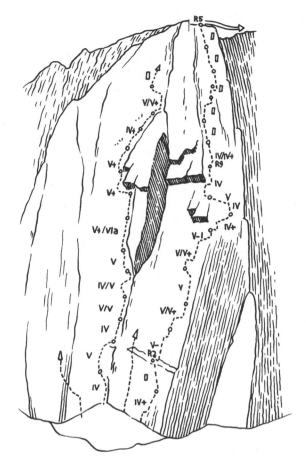

3.11 A 'topo' with Alpine grades marked.

Finally, the 'Graded List' is a useful and entertaining adjunct to a grading system – it includes all the climbs of a particular grade arranged in what consensus agrees is their order of difficulty.

Never forget that the grading of climbs is an imperfect science and that in adverse conditions, or if you are having a bad day, even climbs of a very lowly grade can present what seem to be ferocious difficulties.

4

The safety chain

The rope

The rope is both a symbolic and physical link between the members of a climbing party; indeed such a party is often referred to as a 'rope'.

The perfect climbing rope is both strong and sufficiently elastic to absorb the energy of a fall. It is flexible enough to allow secure knots to be formed in it and to be convenient in use, but robust enough to be hard-wearing and to resist cuts and abrasion. Early climbing ropes were made of natural fibres of which hemp was considered to be the most suitable. This fell far short of the ideal, particularly when wet, and in the 1950s synthetic polymers such as nylon began to be widely used for climbing ropes.

The first nylon ropes combined long strands of nylon in a spiral to produce a *hawser-laid rope* (figure 4.1). These are still available and are used in situations where their low price and hard-wearing nature are valuable and where the excellent handling properties of more modern ropes are not required. They give considerable strength and elasticity but are unsuitable for use with most modern belaying devices.

Almost all modern climbers use ropes of *kernmantel* construction (figure 4.1) in which bundles of parallel fibres of nylon are enclosed in a hard-wearing woven sheath. This construction gives a rope which is less prone to twisting than the hawser-laid construction with improved handling and 'knottability'.

Choosing a rope

The most important characteristic of the rope is that it is capable of absorbing the energy of a fall. You may climb for a lifetime without ever taking a long leader fall, but if you do fall it is vitally important that your rope has the right characteristics. Sheer strength is only part of the picture. We could climb on wire hawser – which would never break – but anyone taking a long fall would be subject to such violent forces when the rope brought them to a sudden stop that serious injury would be inevitable.

The simplest way to ensure that you are buying a rope with the right characteristics is to buy one that is UIAA (Union Internationale des

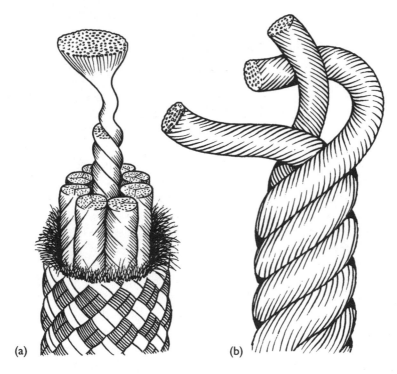

(a)   (b)

4.1 (a) Kernmantel rope. (b) Hawser-laid rope.

Associations Alpines) approved. The UIAA subjects ropes to a regime that tests their strength, energy absorption, knottability and abrasion resistance. UIAA approval confirms that the rope has exceeded high standards in all these areas. They approve two categories of rope: full ropes and half ropes. *Full ropes* are generally about 11mm (⅖ in) in diameter with a static breaking load well in excess of 2 tonnes. They are intended to be used as the sole link between individual members of a climbing party – *single rope*. In contrast, *half ropes* are thinner (generally about 9mm (⅜in) in diameter) and with a static breaking load of around 1.8 tonnes. As their name implies, they are intended to be used as half of a *double rope* system. As explained in Chapter 5, climbing on double ropes gives more versatility and more security on complex pitches and doubles the distance the party could descend by abseil, which is a significant feature on major alpine climbs. Ropes are most commonly sold in lengths of 45m (145ft) and 50m (165ft). Unless you are climbing in an area where pitches are unusually long a 45m (145ft) rope is usually sufficient. Fifty-metre (165ft) double ropes are widely used in alpine climbing.

On climbs up to about Severe standard there is generally little need for double ropes. They are much more valuable as climbs become more complex except in certain areas where climbs tend to follow straight crack lines, such as in the Yosemite Valley, and here single ropes may be used even on the hardest climbs. If you are starting to climb with an experienced climber who uses double ropes, then in due course it may be a good idea for you to acquire something similar, but usually single ropes are more suitable for use by beginners.

You can choose from a wide range of colours which help to avoid confusion when more than one rope is uncoiled on a ledge. Some ropes are treated with water-repellent coatings but I would not consider the extra price of these to be worthwhile except for people who expect to do a great deal of winter or alpine climbing.

Ropes vary in their handling qualities. Before buying one, check that a knot can be formed snugly in the rope and get a feel for how easily the rope will clip into karabiners. When you have found a rope that is UIAA approved, has the kind of handling that you like and a colour that matches your tights, then you can probably go ahead and buy it – but remember to check that the rope is a full rope or half rope as you require. Full ropes are marked (1) and half ropes (1/2) at each end. I have always bought my own ropes from one of the big manufacturers and have tended to avoid cheaper models, though I am sure that these are entirely safe.

Static ropes

Some ropes manufactured for mountain rescue purposes or for use in yachting are very similar in appearance to kernmantel climbing ropes but are dramatically different in performance. Such ropes are made of Terylene and are constructed to be of low stretch and low energy absorption to allow efficient hoisting. These are static ropes rather than the dynamic ropes used in climbing. On no account climb on them; their effect is rather like the wire hawser described earlier. Static ropes can be suitable in nuts and other items of equipment where dynamic properties are unnecessary.

Rope care

Ropes are astonishingly strong. I once worked at a climbing school which had a weight-drop machine to give people practice by dropping a weight of about 60kg (130lb) to be held by a belaying climber. One day, we found the oldest and most damaged rope that we possibly could – one that had been retired from active climbing for several years and had seen its share of towing cars and so on. The rope was so damaged that the sheath had parted in several places but the rope sustained dozens of simulated severe falls without breaking.

However, when climbers' lives are at stake, you want to ensure that the rope is in the best possible condition. Ropes are also too expensive to be neglected.

Keeping ropes in good condition:

- Always run the rope through your hands as you uncoil it at the bottom of a climb and as you coil it at the top, checking for any damage, irregularities or abrasion.
- When ropes are on the ground or on a ledge, avoid standing on them as this can cause cuts against sharp edges.
- Try to avoid putting the rope in positions where it will be exposed to grit and other abrasive substances.
- Nylon is a relatively simple chemical compound and is damaged by ultraviolet light and chemicals such as battery acid.
- After use, hang ropes in a cool, dry place out of direct sunlight and from time to time hand-wash them with mild soap and warm water to get rid of any embedded grit.

Some manufacturers recommend that a rope should be taken out of serious use two years after manufacture even if it has never been climbed on. Few climbers would follow this advice, although organizations such as Outward Bound have to. For my own climbing I have always inspected my ropes regularly and carefully.

Retire a rope if:

- It has held a serious fall (say more than 10m/33ft).
- It has become excessively stiff.
- It shows any significant local damage or a generally high level of abrasion.

Though ropes are enormously strong, even in abnormal use or extreme situations, the two abuses that they cannot cope with are being cut and being melted. Once, whilst practising a mountain rescue manoeuvre, I abseiled down to a climber who, feigning injury, was hanging free from a jammed rope. To complete the 'rescue' I had to attach a new rope to his harness and then cut the jammed rope, which was bearing all his weight, with a sharp knife. I had barely applied the edge of the knife to the 11mm (⅜in) rope on which he was suspended when it parted with a horrifyingly sudden 'ping'. Now I am sure that you will not be careless with knives during a climb, but some crags have rock flakes with extremely sharp edges. It is vital that your rope management prevents the rope from running near such an edge. There was a serious accident on a climb called Sassenach on Ben Nevis a number of years ago when a climber, using a single rope, slipped when above a sharp-edged chockstone. The rope was cut and the climber killed.

Heat generated by friction is the other major threat to your rope. On no account must a moving loaded rope be allowed to pass over another static rope. If this happens, the heat generated will cause the stationary rope to melt in seconds.

Coiling a rope

Coiling a rope both stores it neatly and, if done properly, allows the rope to be conveniently uncoiled for use. A badly coiled rope is an abomination which can easily take ten minutes to untangle. Two main methods exist: the climber's coil and the rucksack coil. Before starting either, you should run the entire length of the rope through your hands and 'flake' it out by dropping it in random coils on the ground.

Climber's coil

To make a climber's coil (figure 4.2):

---

1. Take the upper end of the flaked rope in your left hand and extend both arms to measure the length of the first loop of the coil.
2. Bring your hands together and pass the rope from your right hand to your left imparting a slight twist to counteract the natural twisting tendency of the rope.
3. Repeat the process, gradually building up the number of coils held in your left hand.
4. Stop when you have about 4m (13ft) of rope still uncoiled.
5. Turn about 30cm (12in) of the initial end of the rope back on itself to form a bight (a bend) and then tightly wind the long, remaining end of the rope around this and all the coils, working towards the loop formed by the bight.
6. When you have about 20cm (8in) of rope left, tuck this through the loop formed by the bight and, using the initial end of the rope, pull it tight. You should now have a secure climber's coil.

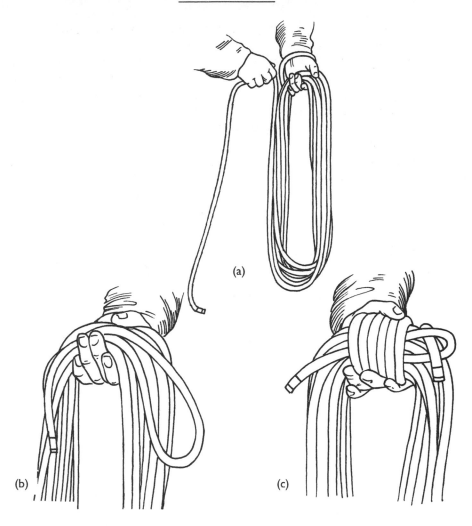

(a)

(b)

(c)

4.2 Making a climber's coil. (a) Forming the coils. (b) Starting the lashing. (c) Ready to tighten and finish the lashing.

To uncoil this, reverse the process exactly and, after undoing the initial lashing, remove one coil at a time. Do not be tempted to put the coils on the ground and simply pull the rope off from them as this almost always results in a complicated tangle.

Making a climber's coil is a satisfying process, though it sometimes tends to put twists into the rope. Some people form the coils by sitting on the ground with knees apart and use this position as a former for the coils. It is a convenient way of coiling a rope for general use.

Rucksack coil

This allows the rope to be carried on the climber's back and so is very useful if some unroped scrambling has to be done before the rope is uncoiled. It also appears to put fewer twists in the rope than the climber's coil, so I tend to use it when storing my ropes.

Making a rucksack coil (figure 4.3):

---

1. Start by finding both ends of the rope, then flake these onto the ground and work backwards to the mid-point of the rope.
2. You are aiming to coil the rope doubled, by laying folds into your left hand.
3. Stop when you have reached a point where about 6m (20ft) of the double rope remains uncoiled, and hold the coils from their mid-point in your left hand.
4. Take the uncoiled end of the rope and wind it several times around the folded coils.
5. To finish, pass a bight of the uncoiled rope through the loop at the head of the coils and turn it back on itself to form a doll's head coil and two long tails about 180cm (6ft) in length.
6. The rope is slung on your back, the tails crossed over the coils on your back and tied with a reef knot at the front to complete the process.

All this is rather easier than it sounds and is probably the fastest of all methods of coiling.

Quick-release coils

Various other methods exist. If you want a rope to be very rapidly available for use, then you can use chain coils or can simply feed the rope into a rucksack, starting with one end and then identifying the 'top' end by tying it to the rucksack strap. With luck, when you pull on the top end, the whole rope will come out of your rucksack in a helpful way.

Knots
Roping up

There is a wide variety of knots and many of these can be safely used in climbing. My own philosophy is to have the minimum repertoire of knots necessary to undertake a climb but to know these knots so well that if necessary they could be tied in the dark and in a blizzard!

Knots are best learnt by following a diagram with a length of rope in your hands or, even better, by having someone who knows the knot

4.3 Making a rucksack coil. (a) Forming the coils in the double rope. (b) Forming the doll's head lashing. (c) Carrying the rope.

showing you with one rope while you imitate with another. All knots work most effectively when they are snugged down and look neat. This is particularly so with figure-of-eight knots and you should try to avoid extraneous twists whilst tying the knot.

Figure-of-eight knots

The figure-of-eight knot (and its variants) in figure 4.4 is probably the most simple and most versatile knot in climbing. It is not always the

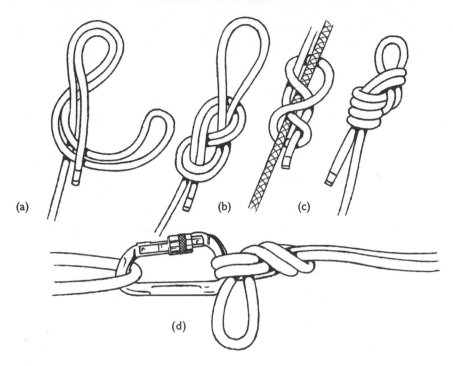

4.4 (a) Simple figure-of-eight loop. (b) Fisherman's knot. (c) Figure-of-eight loop with fisherman's knot stopper. (d) Figure-of-eight tied back into a screwgate karabiner.

most elegant solution, but if you know this family of knots you can deal with most situations.

The simplest form of a figure-of-eight loop is tied by making a bight with the last 50–60cm (20–24in) of the rope and then tying the figure-of-eight knot as shown in figure 4.4. If the rope is soft and in good condition it will form a secure and snug knot and as long as you leave a tail of about 10cm (4in) the knot will be sufficient in itself.

If you have any doubts about the knot loosening itself (this would generally happen if the rope was too stiff or the knot tied too loosely) then you should use a *stopper knot* to secure the tail. Many climbers use stopper knots all the time on figure-of-eight knots. Others find that they add extra bulk without materially increasing safety. My recommendation is to use them until you have been climbing long enough to make your own decision.

Fisherman's knot

The best stopper knot to use is the fisherman's knot, also known as the *double overhand* or the *grapevine* (figure 4.4). Start with a bight of 80cm

(30in) of rope. Roping up with a figure-of-eight loop tied in the bight is the most simple of tying-on methods and is ideal when the rope is to be attached to your harness with a screwgate karabiner.

Rethreading

If you plan to tie the rope directly into the harness – and I would generally recommend this unless the manufacturer of your harness suggests something different – then you need to tie the figure-of-eight loop in a different way by rethreading. This looks a little mystifying at first but is really very simple once you have got used to what length of rope to leave. A figure-of-eight knot is tied in the single rope (about 1m (3ft) from the end if you are going to add a stopper knot), the long tail is threaded through the harness and then rethreaded following the initial figure-of-eight in its entirety.

Figure-of-eight knots are stronger if tied so that the load rope follows the wider radius in the knot, and more convenient if the loop is only about 10cm (4in) in length.

Bowline

If you forget your harness or are travelling extremely light, you may wish to tie directly onto the climbing rope. It is possible to do this with a rethreaded figure-of-eight, tightening the knot snugly around your waist by manipulating a single strand through the figure-of-eight knot. This is a rather laborious system and there is little doubt that the quickest and most elegant way to tie onto the end of a rope (and one tested by generations of sailors and climbers) is by using the bowline (figure 4.5). This is a superb knot in many respects. It is quick to tie (although not quite as easy for beginners) and does not jam as badly as the figure-of-eight under load. This also constitutes its greatest weakness, since it can all too easily work itself loose when not loaded. For this reason, using the fisherman's knot as a stopper knot is in my opinion absolutely mandatory with the bowline. It is, of course, also possible to tie directly onto a harness using a bowline and stopper knot.

Whatever method you choose, ensure that your tying of the knot is absolutely foolproof. I have cultivated a slight degree of paranoia about knots and I check both my tie-on knot and the buckle of my harness at the start of every pitch. It has not come undone yet but it is better to be sure than sorry.

Knots for joining

We will look in detail at equipment a little later, but since we are tuned to knots we should also consider the knots that are used to join ropes or

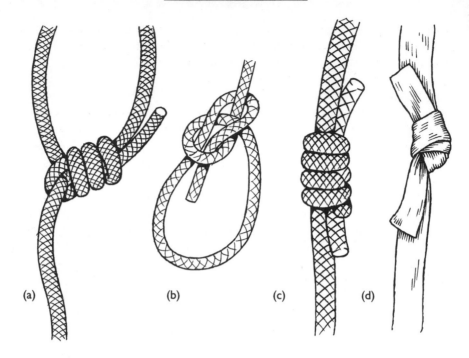

(a)   (b)   (c)   (d)

4.5 (a) Bowline and stopper. (b) Bowline without stopper. (c) Double fisherman's knot. (d) Tape knot.

climbing webbing. This is mainly done in order to make slings or runners (knotted loops with a great variety of applications).

Joining ropes

The best, indeed almost the only, knot for joining ropes is the *double fisherman's knot* (figure 4.5). As its name suggests, this is two adjoining fisherman's knots. With a tail of 10cm (4in) extending out of a well-tightened knot, this is an extremely reliable joining knot both for slings and for joining two ropes for abseiling.

Joining webbing (tape)

Climbing webbing is very versatile when used for slings. It is comfortable to carry and its thinness allows it to be used behind flakes or spikes that are only very slightly separated from the rock. Webbing, however, is more prone to damage by abrasion and ultraviolet light than the equivalent strength of kernmantel rope so it is good practice to recycle your webbing equipment reasonably frequently. The best slings are probably those that are bought ready-looped and joined by bar-tacked stitching, but this is expensive and sooner or later you will want a sling of a particular size. For this you will need to use the right knot.

You can use the double fisherman's knot (figure 4.5) but this is a little bulky. Most commonly used is the so-called *tape knot* or *water knot*, which is simply an overhand knot rethreaded in the opposite direction (figure 4.5). This knot puts the maximum area of tape in contact and provides good strength. Unfortunately, the ends of the knot can migrate with uncanny ease and so you must leave at least 10cm (4in) of tail extending out of the knot, and check it frequently in use. Most importantly of all, you need to load the knot before use and indeed this is good practice after tying any slings. This is best done by attaching one end of the sling to an anchor or the branch of a tree and jumping actively in the loop.

Belays – holding a fall

The term 'belay' must have confused more than a few beginners since it can apply equally to the anchor, the process of attachment to an anchor and the process of securing the rope of your companion. Thus, you could belay yourself to a belay in order to belay your partner. If you understand this gobbledegook, then you have definitely arrived as a climber!

When a fall is held, a force – the *impact force* – builds up throughout the safety chain and will affect all its component parts. These include the person who is falling, the rope, the knots, the belayer, the karabiners and the anchor (figure 4.6).

The traditional way of holding a fall is by the body belay (see page 63) but this has been largely superseded by the use of various belay devices. I strongly recommend that you use a belay device in your own climbing.

Belay devices

These work by developing friction on a loaded rope to allow the belayer to arrest a fall without having to apply undue force. They are generally slotted metal *belay plates* or divided metal tubes (figure 4.7), but friction brakes originally designed for abseiling – such as the figure-of-eight *descender* – are also used as belay devices.

The moving climber's rope is paid out or taken in through the belay device and the screwgate karabiner with which it is attached to the belayer's harness. You should use a heavy-duty screwgate karabiner that is of round section and of at least 2000kg (4400lb) rated strength. I like the large pear-shaped karabiners that are available.

4.6 The climber is tied on to a 'bombproof' spike anchor via a doubled supertape sling and screwgate karabiner. He is attached to the anchor by a simple figure-of-eight knot in his rope and to his belaying companion with a belay plate. He is well–positioned and tight on the anchor.

The karabiner is attached either to the tie-on loop in the rope or to a suitably strong part of the harness. The climber's rope to be controlled is passed through the device and clipped into the karabiner.

When rope is fed out or taken in, the belay plate tends to sit a few centimetres from the karabiner and gives relatively little friction. A retaining cord or wire is generally used to prevent the plate migrating down the bight of rope, although in practice this does not seem to be much of a problem.

The rope running to the climber is called the *live rope* or *active rope*; the other is the *dead rope* or *control rope*. In the event of a fall or if the climber's weight comes onto the live rope, the belayer pulls the dead rope in the direction opposite to the pull on the live rope. This forces the belay plate against the karabiner and generates enough friction to stop the fall.

Depending on their design and the type of rope used, belay devices (figure 4.7) will usually generate between 200 and 400 kg (440–880lb) of braking force on the rope. In the event of a very severe fall such as one of fall factor 2 (see Chapter 8) generating a force in the rope in excess of this, then some rope will slip through the plate. This is, in fact, a very desirable design feature because it means that for holding simple falls there is no slippage, but for more severe falls the plate will automatically provide a degree of slip to reduce the impact force on the system.

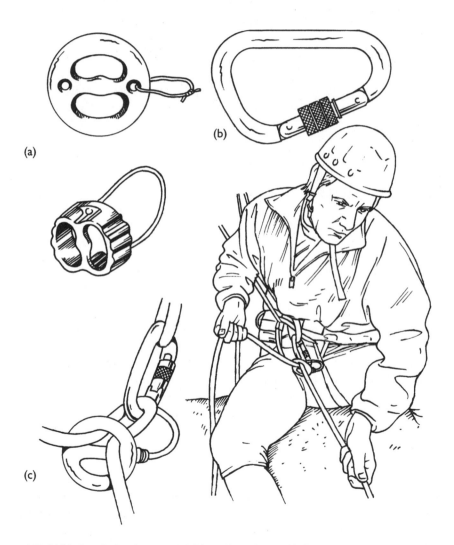

4.7 (a) Various belay devices and (b) HMS karabiner. (c) The rope locked by the brake hand to hold a second's fall.

When belaying another climber's rope, you should be constantly aware of where the pull of any force will come and ensure that you are able to apply the opposite braking force with your control hand on the dead rope. It is vital that the dead rope is under control at all times. Normally, you aim to have one hand on the live rope and one on the dead rope. If you must scratch your nose or take a photograph you may let go of the live rope but on no account remove the control hand from the dead rope. When climbers fall they usually inform their belayer, (figure 4.7) often by some rather urgent non-verbal communication, but some falls occur without warning – particularly those where a hold has broken. If your hand is not firmly on the dead rope you will not hold such a fall. When warned that a leader fall is imminent, I tend to make doubly sure by applying both hands to the dead rope.

You will find it worthwhile to develop a conscious system of both taking in and paying out rope without removing the control hand from its proper position.

The body belay

In the traditional manner, the live rope is passed around the waist above the attachment point to the anchor (figure 4.8). The live rope at the front of the body passes through one hand; a turn of the dead rope is taken around the wrist of the other hand. In the event of a fall, both hands are brought across the body to increase the angle through which the rope is turning. This provides considerable friction and will arrest a fall. (It is also called a *waist belay*.)

The advantages of this system are that it is quick and relatively simple to set up and it allows the rope to be taken in rapidly on easy ground. It also makes it easy to provide a 'dynamic arrest' by deliberately slipping the rope. This is sometimes of value in winter climbing when suspect anchors are in use.

However, its disadvantages are that it applies a much greater strain to the belayer who, for a fall of any severity, must be well clothed and wearing gloves. Finally, the worst aspect of using a body belay is that it applies a twisting force to the belayer which in the worst case can cause the rope to be dropped.

Most modern harnesses have a front attachment point and, in order to prevent this twisting action, it is usually necessary to attach yourself to the anchor via a secondary tie-on at the back of the harness. I do not recommend the use of body belays until you have had sufficient experience of climbing to recognize the circumstances in which they might be used and the limitations that would then apply.

Munter hitch

The Munter hitch or *Italian hitch* is a simple arrangement of the rope through a karabiner which provides the correct degree of friction to lower a climber or hold a fall (figure 4.8). It would be my first choice if I dropped my belay plate, but it must only be used with a screwgate karabiner. Its disadvantage is that it is slightly more awkward to pay out and take in rope than with a belay plate and also the technique has a tendency to put twists into the slack rope.

At first sight it would appear that the hitch would apply dangerous friction from a running rope to a stationary rope but in fact all parts of the hitch are moving simultaneously. Although there may be momentary fusing of the sheath in the event of a severe fall, it is a safe, if slightly inconvenient, method to use. The hitch should be tied so that the live rope is nearest to the back bar of the karabiner, and in such a way that if the climber fell the movement of the rope would tend to tighten the locking gate of the karabiner.

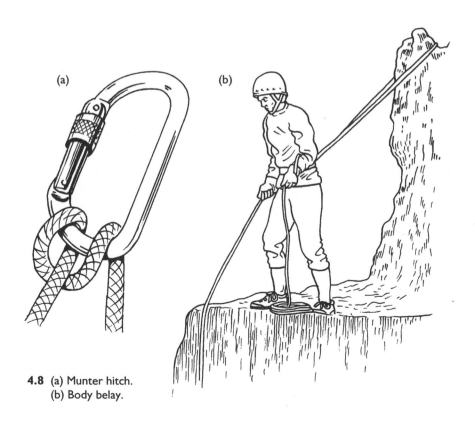

(a)

(b)

4.8 (a) Munter hitch.
(b) Body belay.

Attachment to anchors

Whichever method of belaying the rope is used, a severe fall will put a considerable force on the belayer. As belayer, you must be correctly positioned to withstand this and must be attached to suitable anchors so that you are not pulled from the stance.

Any strong force applied by the live rope on the belayer will tend to move the belayer and the anchors into a straight line. If not already standing or sitting in this straight line, the belayer will be moved with some suddenness. This increases the chance of not holding the rope securely and, more importantly, increases the shock loading on the anchors.

Similarly, if the belayer is tied to the anchors by a slack attachment, then in the event of a fall this will be suddenly tightened, applying a substantial and dangerous jerk to the anchor. Therefore correct positioning (figures 4.6 and 4.9) is absolutely vital.

In order to get as near to the straight-line position as possible, it is often a good idea to sit on a belay ledge with anchors above you and in any case this is the most stable position. Sometimes it is preferable to belay on a small ledge with good high anchors, rather than on a larger ledge with poorly positioned low anchors, particularly if these are nuts which could be lifted out with an upward pull. On difficult climbs, stances are sometimes little more than a foothold and here it is vital that good anchors are used and that the lead climber places runners as soon as possible.

Choosing the correct position is made more difficult because the direction of the likely force can change as the climber moves up a pitch or will depend on whether a running belay holds or is pulled out. However, it is still possible to make the best decision as to your position, if necessary moving during the course of a long pitch.

Also, particularly at the top of climbs, it is sometimes necessary to use an anchor that is a long way back from the point where you want to position yourself. Ideally you should position yourself where you can see the other member of the party – and this is essential if your companion is relatively inexperienced.

A fall held through a runner will tend to lift the belayer from a ledge by applying an upward force, but the most severe fall (which is fall factor 2) would be experienced if the leader fell without a runner in place or if a runner had been placed and failed. Here the climber would fall beneath the belayer and apply a very strong downward force. It is this downward force that you should have in mind when attaching yourself to an anchor. In comparison with such severe falls, holding a second on the pitch below you rarely presents great difficulties to a well-positioned belayer.

4.9 A well-positioned belayer. The load on the rope caused by a second's fall is in a direct line with the belayer's attachment to the anchor. The belayer's sitting position adds to his stability.

Tying-on to an anchor

Assume, for the time being, that the anchor exists. It might be a firm attachment to the mountain or a sling around a massive tree and it culminates in a karabiner, preferably one of the screwgate variety. For your own security and that of your companion it is important that you know how to secure yourself to this anchor.

By far the simplest method – one that served me very well for the first five years of my climbing is to tie a figure-of-eight knot in a bight of the main climbing rope and clip this loop into the karabiner (see figure 4.6). You are now secure, particularly if the karabiner is a screwgate and you have remembered to lock the gate. For your own security on a ledge, you require little more. The difficulties arise if you are belaying the rope of your companion to protect them against a fall.

Unless you are climbing with double ropes the figure-of-eight method is difficult to use for more than one anchor and it is awkward to adjust if you are more than a metre or so from your anchor point. It is good practice to use more than one anchor point for your main belay to provide insurance against the failure of one of its component parts and to use screwgate karabiners.

The clove hitch

The clove hitch (figure 4.10) can be used instead. The only advantages that this offers over the simple figure-of-eight is its ease of adjustment and the fact that it is less likely to jam under load. This is my method of choice when climbing on double ropes using one rope clove-hitched to each of two anchors.

Tied-back clove hitch

This is a good method of belaying to a distant anchor but does require the climber to carry an extra screwgate karabiner attached to the harness. The rope is clipped through the distant anchor and the climber then takes up position. The rope running back from the anchor is attached with a clove hitch to a spare screwgate karabiner attached to the strong point of the harness. The hitch (figure 4.10) can be easily adjusted to get exactly the correct length between the climber and the anchor.

If a second anchor is used which is within reach, the main rope emerging from the first clove hitch can be clove-hitched directly into the karabiner of the second anchor. If the second anchor is more distant, then it too is clipped through and the rope tied back to the climber with a clove hitch. This ideally should involve a second screwgate karabiner but if this is not available two snaplinks with reversed gates may be used instead.

Tied-back figure-of-eight

The most versatile method of belaying, but perhaps the most laborious, is the tied-back figure-of-eight (see figure 4.4). Imagine that you have two anchors, one about 3m (10ft) from where you intend to position yourself, the other 1m (3ft). You are climbing on a single rope. Clip your main rope through the karabiner on the distant anchor and walk back to where you intend to stand. Take a half step back towards the distant anchor, thread the bight of the main rope through your own tie-on knot and tie a figure-of-eight in the bight. Retrace your half step from the distant anchor and you will be attached with a tight link to it. Now take the main rope emerging from your tied-back figure-of-eight and attach it to the nearer anchor with a clove hitch, adjusting this to be tight also. You are now independently loading both anchors and are correctly positioned. If no second anchor is used, the tail on the bight of the tied-back figure-of-eight must be about 25cm (10in) in length. If you really want to show off, thread the bight through your main tie-on knot and then

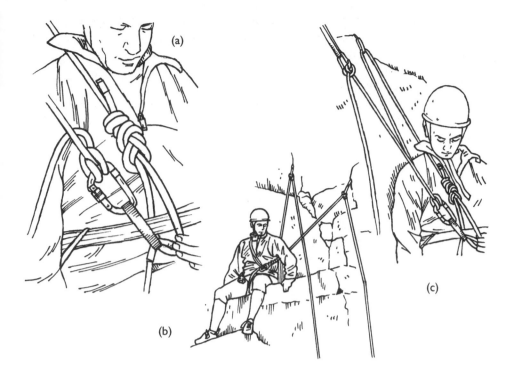

4.10 (a) Tied-back clove hitch. (b) Clove-hitched to two anchors when using double ropes. (c) Tied-back clove hitch plus direct clove hitch to use two anchors with a single rope. See figure 4.14 for example of clove hitch.

measure it to the second anchor before tying the tied-back figure-of-eight. If you have allowed the right quantity of rope, you can then clip the tail of the knot into your secondary anchor. This is elegant but requires practice.

By regarding the main rope emerging from your tied-back figure-of-eight as your starting point, you can repeat the process and include as many anchor points as you wish. However, you will find that you quickly run out of rope! In practice, this main method will cover most situations if you extend or link different anchor points with suitably strong webbing slings.

Remember, the aim is to load multiple anchors simultaneously and independently and not sequentially.

Communication

It is important that each member of the climbing party knows what the others are up to. This is especially true in relation to whether an individual is or is not being protected by the rope. Various systems of communication have developed to allow this vital information to pass between climbers even when wind and weather intervene.

The British system:

---

1. As leader, you arrive at the top of a pitch and secure yourself to the mountain. You shout, '*Taking in.*' This tells the second, belaying below, that the leader is secure and that the second can now remove the rope from the belay plate.
2. Having done this, the second shouts, '*Take in.*' The leader duly pulls in the rope hand over hand. Note that when this is happening, the second is not protected by the leader and therefore must remain attached to the anchor.
3. When the slack rope is fully pulled in by the leader and comes tight on the second, the second shouts, '*That's me.*' This tells the leader that the rope is tight to the second and you can now put the rope into your belay plate.
4. With the second's rope securely held in your belay plate, you can now hold a fall and inform the second of this by shouting '*Climb when you're ready.*'
5. The second can now safely untie from the anchor and shouts, '*Climbing.*'
6. The leader acknowledges by shouting, '*Okay,*' and the second can now proceed up the pitch.
7. Whilst on the pitch, if the second needs more rope (for instance to make a downward step) he shouts, '*Slack.*' If there is too much slack between him and the leader he shouts '*Take in.*' And so the party proceeds.

On a short pitch and on a calm sunny day, communication is easy and an experienced party may use an abbreviated version. However, in adverse conditions it is very important to stick to this agreed sequence of calls, because often you can only hear the rhythm of the calls. Similarly, avoid extraneous comments that will only confuse the other person. On a windy day, a soliloquy from the leader about the difficulty of finding an anchor or the magnificence of the view will only confuse the anxious second.

When both climbers are on the same ledge it has always seemed to me rather unnecessary to use this formal system for communication, though some people do insist on it.

Different countries have different approaches and in the USA the system is admirably concise, consisting of each climber using 'On belay' and 'Off belay' to indicate their status.

Sometimes, particularly when it is very windy, it is impossible to hear the signals from the other end of the rope. In those conditions it is wise to arrange a system of tugs on the rope. Since the single most important signal is the one which tells the second that it is safe to climb, I tend to use a system where three strong tugs on the rope means: 'Climb when you're ready.' This seems to work well, but it is perhaps worth pointing out to the second that a single very strong pull should not be ignored – it means you have fallen off!

Protection equipment

Climbers carry a range of equipment which enables them to arrange secure anchors both for belay stances and for use as running belays. This next section looks at the karabiners, slings, nuts and other equipment that are used in this way.

Karabiners ('krabs', 'biners' or 'clips')

When I start to lead a pitch, I would normally expect to be carrying a total of between 12 and 30 karabiners. They are hugely versatile and essential to most modern forms of climbing. All karabiners (figure 4.11) consist of an approximately oval loop of metal to which access is gained by a springloaded gate. It is still possible to obtain steel karabiners but in almost all cases aluminium alloy is now more suitable and is certainly much more widely available.

Locking karabiners

Here a sleeve, which can be operated manually or sometimes by a springloaded mechanism, can lock the gate of the karabiner in a closed position. The most common mechanism for the manual form of locking karabiner is a threaded sleeve, so the term 'screwgate' is almost a synonym for locking karabiner. The gate is part of the design of a karabiner that weakens its strength. By having a locking gate the strength of the karabiner is increased somewhat but its main value is in preventing the gate opening and the rope escaping from the confines of the karabiner. Therefore, locking karabiners are used in situations where great security is desirable, such as in the attachment of a climber to the climbing rope or as the culminating point of a main anchor. A typical test load for such a karabiner is 2200kg (4850lb).

The versions with a springloaded sleeve will lock automatically on closure. In some situations this is a great advantage but I prefer the manual closure for most forms of climbing because it offers the reassuring possibility of tightening the gate up quite firmly against the pressure that might arise from a moving rope.

I once had a close escape in the Himalayas when abseiling on fixed ropes using a springloaded locking karabiner which sprang open in use. If I had been more alert I would have arranged the rope to run in a direction that closed the gate rather than opened it, but this experience has rather jaundiced my view of this piece of equipment. Properly used, they are of course entirely safe, but any piece of equipment has limitations.

The strongest karabiners are D-shaped as this brings the load close to its strongest part – the back bar. However, for reasons of convenience other forms also exist such as the pear-shaped karabiner, which is very convenient for use with a belay plate.

Snaplinks

On a typical rock climb I would expect to carry perhaps three or four screwgate karabiners and maybe 20 or 25 snaplinks (figure 4.11). They are much lighter than screwgate karabiners and are much more convenient for clipping the rope in and out.

Their disadvantages are that, because the gate is unsecured, only a light spring prevents the rope from unclipping accidentally. Also, although the strength of snaplinks for a pull along the line of the back bar can be comparable with that of screwgates, they are very much weaker for a crosswise pull that includes the relatively weak gate.

Kilopond and kilonewton

Just to confuse you, because in physics and engineering a kilogram is actually a measure of mass rather than force, the test force of karabiners is now more commonly expressed in *kiloponds* (kp) or *kilonewtons* (kn). For example I have an American karabiner with a longitudinal strength rated at 21kn with the gate closed and 5.7kn with the gate open. For practical purposes, you can assume that a kilopond is the same as a kilogram weight and that a kilonewton is equivalent to 100kg (220lb) weight.

Choice of shape

If you go into any climbing shop you are likely to see a wide range of karabiners. The best general-purpose ones are probably the D-shaped or offset-D types. This type of karabiner brings the load close to the back bar of the karabiner, where it is strongest, and the offset form gives more width at one end and allows a wider opening of the gate when clipping in.

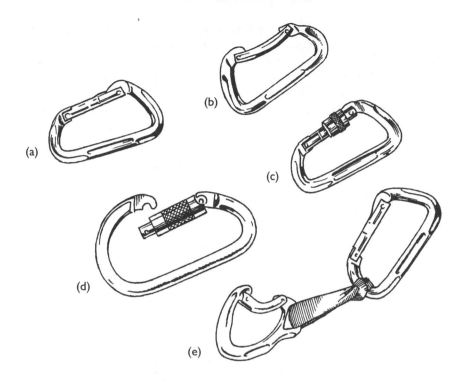

4.11 Offset-D karabiners with (a) straight-gate snaplink, (b) bent-gate snaplink and (c) screwgate. (d) HMS screwgate belay karabiner. (e) Specialist quick-draw and snaplink combination for high-speed 'clips' on bolt routes.

Oval karabiners, which are symmetrical in form, are popular in *aid climbing* (using equipment for direct progress rather than simply for protection) because they do not shift under load, but they tend to be less strong for a particular weight of material.

Karabiners with a slight beak at the nose are easier to clip into items of equipment and light springs allow the rope to be clipped in much more easily (though of course this increases the danger of the rope popping out).

There are advantages in having most of your karabiners of a similar design, because you will then become extremely familiar with their ergonomics. I would recommend using medium-to-lightweight Ds or offset-Ds, but also carrying a small number of more heavyweight snaplinks for use on particularly vital runners or heavyweight slings. If you run out of screwgate krabs, use two similar snaplinks with their gates opposed.

When using karabiners you must avoid putting them in situations where:

- The back bar is levered across an edge.
- Snaplinks are subjected to a three-way force.
- The gate may open by being pressed against the rock in the event of a fall.
- Two snaplinks are clipped together – they may twist and open each other.

Most of these problems can be avoided by judicious use of extenders and screwgate karabiners.

Slings

These are loops of nylon webbing (tape) or rope. For most climbing, tape slings are ubiquitous and are usually carried looped over the shoulder in either single or double lengths, a single length having a circumference of 120cm (4ft) and double length a circumference of 240cm (8ft). Tubular tape in 2.5 or 1.5cm (1 or ⅝in) widths is convenient in use but flat woven 'supertape' is very much stronger. Shorter tape slings of about 10cm (4in) in length are sometimes called *'quick-draws'* and are often used as extensions to runners. The only common use of rope slings is in prusik loops, which are generally made from 5 or 6mm (⅛ or ¼ in) kernmantel rope (see Chapter 8).

Anchors
Spikes and blocks

Solidly attached spikes or massive detached blocks of rock can be used as anchors. A heavyweight tape sling is put over the spike or block, either single or double as its size permits. Alternatively, the climbing rope can be passed around the spike or block and tied into the harness with a tied-back figure-of-eight. Spikes and blocks are at their best when used to anchor a climber who is positioned below them as this minimizes the danger of the rope lifting off. Sometimes this danger can be lessened if the spike or block is treated as a crack, and a nut or camming device is used instead. Check carefully to make sure that the block or spike is firmly attached to the mountain.

For small features, this is best done by tapping with the heel of the hand and listening for a tell-tale dull note. *Cinching* a sling by tying it in a lark's foot (see figure 4.14 on page 78) weakens it considerably but is sometimes useful to hold a sling in place on a poorly formed spike.

Threads

A thread occurs when a natural tunnel in the rock or two adjacent blocks or a securely jammed chockstone allows a sling or rope to be threaded to form an anchor. Threads are much more secure against upward pulls than a spike or block. Normally a sling is threaded through and the ends joined with a karabiner. For both block and thread belays, a screwgate karabiner should be used if there is any danger of a three-way pull. It is in any case good practice to use one or two screwgate karabiners in a particular belay. Avoid (or pad) threads that have rope-cutting sharp edges and watch out for the sling jamming on removal. Beware of threads where one side is actually a loose block which would easily move under load.

Nuts

In the 1930s climbers experimented with inserting small pebbles into cracks to use as threads. Eventually, metal machine nuts with their threads removed began to be used and these began to evolve into purpose-made devices of various shapes and materials but the dominant shapes were the wedge and the hexagon and aluminium alloy was the preferred material (figure 4.12).

The concept of the nut is very simple. Find a point at which a crack narrows and select a nut that will wedge above the narrowing. Modern nuts equipped with wire slings may hold a downward load of up to 1.5 tonnes in a good placement but can be removed with a gentle upward pull. The skill lies in spotting the placement and in selecting the nut that will make best use of it. Good placements are in sound and massive rock rather than loose or fragile flakes and have the maximum area of the nut in contact with the rock. Generally speaking, the larger the nut for a given placement, the better.

Most manufacturers make a range of sizes of a particular nut and each nut within the set will have at least two different aspects that can be jammed. I recommend that your main range is made by a single manufacturer because the sizes are then logically graded – for example if a number 5 seems slightly small then you know that a number 6 will be a good fit. At the lowest end of the range, some specialist nuts are only 1 or 2mm (less than $\frac{1}{10}$in) in thickness; at the upper end are huge tube chocks of 10, 15 or 20cm (4, 6 or 8in) in width. The most useful range is between about 3mm and 5cm ($\frac{1}{10}$ and 2in), but the useful range does vary according to the rock type on which you are climbing. After a while you will develop a very good eye and will look at a crack and unerringly select the correct nut to fit. This is very good for saving strength and patience as well as being a satisfying piece of expertise.

The majority of nuts are equipped with wire slings but it is useful to have some of the larger sizes equipped with rope, especially some of the modern Kevlar-based ropes that are extremely strong.

I recommend that for your first set of equipment you stick to one of the classic, slightly curved wedge patterns with perhaps a small number of nuts of the asymmetrical hexagonal type and avoid the more exotic shapes. No matter what shape of nut you use, sooner or later you will find the perfect placement for it and the classic example of this is on Kaisergebirge Wall in the Llanberis Pass where a jammed bicycle crank has been in place for many years and has held many leader falls.

Nuts can also be placed very effectively in narrowings in horizontal cracks or between two *nubbins* of rock. If you cannot find the correct nut to fit a crack, then *in extremis* it is possible to stack two or more nuts in the same crack, but I do not recommend this for main anchors.

Removal of nuts

Subtlety almost always pays greater dividends than brute force! First look at the placement and decide how the nut was placed and then try to manoeuvre it out along the same route. If it is gripping the crack too tightly to move, then give it a tap with a karabiner in order to break its hold and try again. If all else fails, jerk the nut violently in the direction that appears to loosen it, but once it is loose, go back to subtle manoeuvring. Some climbers carry purpose-made nut removal tools which can be applied to recalcitrant nuts. It is an unpleasant blight on a crag to leave rusting wire slings and decaying tapes in place.

Nuts are at their least useful in parallel-sided or flared cracks. Some success can be had by camming the asymmetric hexagons, but this difficulty has now largely been met by the invention of purpose-built camming devices.

Camming devices

Most modern camming devices (figure 4.13) consist of springloaded cams that press against the side of a crack. They are at their best in parallel-sided cracks, but can even be used in flares. The harder they are loaded, the harder they grip. Their invention in the late 1970s transformed hard rock climbing and it is difficult to imagine how we managed without them.

Camming devices are absolutely brilliant but are not without their problems. They are extremely expensive, they are bulkier and heavier than nuts and they require more care in both placement and removal.

A camming device will cover a range of crack sizes and as you work its trigger it will expand and contract across this range. When placed, all the

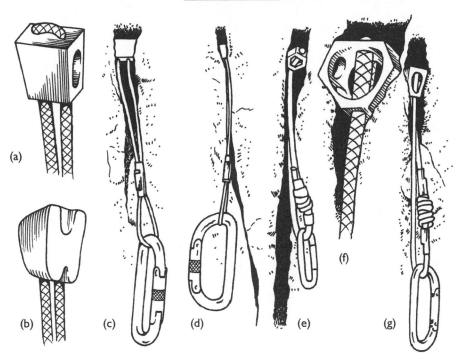

4.12 Nuts: (a+b) wedges on wire; (c) wire placed 'crossways'; (d) secure small wire; (e+f) hexcentrics; (g) wedge on rope in place.

COLEG POWYS - BRECON

cams of the unit must be in contact with the rock. If one or more of the cams are reversed or out of contact with the rock, then the placement is seriously compromised. Near the top of its range it is only just wide enough to fit the crack and if it shifts under load it might move to a slightly wider part of the crack and fail. These devices are at their most reliable in the middle of their range. At their lower size limit they are extremely strong in a good placement but can present considerable diffi-culties in removal simply because they cannot be contracted any further. Removing camming devices that are jammed in this way is an extremely difficult task.

The best placement (figure 4.13) is in a massive crack that is part of the mountain and not just a loose flake attached to it, and at a point that is slightly wider than its immediate surroundings. When placed in the kind of tapered crack that favours the use of nuts, camming devices tend to migrate upwards and I feel they are more convincing in parallel-sided cracks. To minimize migration, use an extension sling to prevent the rope moving the device. Although they are not as good in flared cracks as in parallel ones, everything is a bonus because very few other devices can be used at all. Although placements in flared cracks can be very useful as runners, they can fail unexpectedly and so are best avoided as the central part of main anchors.

Removal of camming devices

Retract the cams and carefully lift the unit from the crack. If it does not lift out readily, proceed with great care. Brute force will almost always result in the device jamming irretrievably and a serious deterioration of your relationship with the person who owns it. When a device is seriously over-cammed and jammed in a crack, then you can sometimes succeed by using a nut removal tool to manoeuvre each cam in turn for a millimetre or so and repeating this time and time again. If this does not succeed, then I have had some success by a devious method involving attaching a chain of karabiners via two small wire nuts to the triggers of the device. Breath suitable invocations and apply a sharp jerk to the karabiner chain. If the gods are smiling on you, the jammed device will pop out. However, prevention is very much better than cure and you should avoid at all costs littering our crags with abandoned ironmongery.

Bolts

Expansion bolts (figure 4.14) inserted in holes drilled in the rock used to be extremely rare except on aid climbing but since the late 1980s they have been widely used in opening up new crags as amenity climbing areas. Many limestone cliffs in France, Spain and Italy have been developed with hundreds of in situ bolts protecting a wide range of climbs ('sport climbing') and similar developments have taken place in desert areas such as the Owens Valley Gorge in eastern California.

Bolt protection allows the climber to concentrate on the rock and the gymnastic possibilities of the route without having to give much thought to placing anchors. The climber simply clips the rope with two karabiners and a short sling into the bolt. Most bolts are secure, but you are placing great trust in the person who installed it in the first place. Avoid placing the karabiner in a way that would allow it to be loaded across its length in the event of a fall, and for a main anchor always use two or more different bolts.

Many climbers are worried about the effect of bolt climbing on some of the more traditional areas of the sport and we will look at these ethical considerations – as well as more on the technique to employ – later in the book.

Pitons

Modern equipment, such as micronuts or camming devices has largely eliminated the need for pitons (figure 4.14) except in winter climbing,

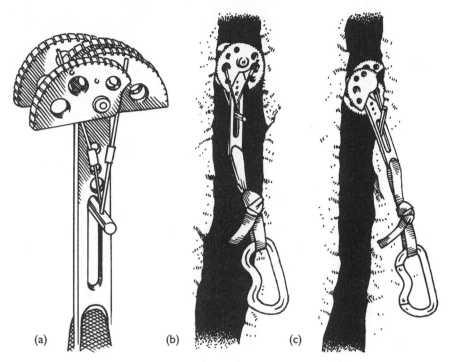

4.13 (a) Camming devices. (b) Well-placed cam and (b) poor placement with one reversed cam.

alpine climbing or the exploration of certain new climbs. When a piton is necessary on a climb, it is usually already in place and it is not usually necessary to carry a piton and the hammer necessary for its insertion. The insertion of pitons is such an infrequent event in modern rock climbing that I consider the techniques to be beyond the scope of this book.

When you do find an *in situ* piton, treat it with some caution. It may have been there many years and, particularly on sea cliffs, may have been subject to corrosion. If an *in situ* piton projects more than 1–2 cm (⅖–¾ in) from the rock, you will reduce leverage by tying it off with a tape sling tied with a clove hitch (strongest) or lark's foot (quickest) (figure 4.14) behind the eye.

Learning to place gear

It requires both imagination and experience to be able to make the most of the security that a particular piece of rock will offer. Every time you use an anchor that someone else has constructed or remove a runner placed by the leader, look carefully at how it has been constructed and

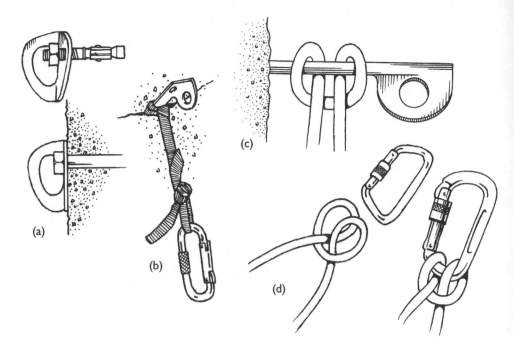

4.14 (a) Bolt. (b) Tied-off blade piton. (c) Lark's foot tie-off. (d) Clove hitch.

what equipment has been used. Your own expertise will grow rapidly as you become tuned to the possibilities of the rock. A particularly good use of a wet afternoon is to find a boulder well equipped with cracks and try to place the entire contents of your 'rack'. Then assess each one in turn for its strength, the direction it can be loaded in and its suitability as a main anchor. If you can get an opinion from a more experienced climber, so much the better.

5

First on the rope

It is a big step from seconding to leading. The leader is at greater risk from a fall and must also find the line of the route on a particular pitch and place any necessary protection. If you are the leader on a long climb you will, in fact, find yourself having to make most of the important decisions about the ascent and calling on qualities of judgement that the second may not often need.

Starting to lead

I still remember my first lead, which was up a ridiculously easy gritstone slab that everyone else at the crag seemed to be using as a descent! Despite this I felt weighed down with the responsibility of it all and what, on a top rope, would have seemed easy was quite challenging enough. You have to adjust to your different situation as a leader. Some people do this very readily, others will take much more time. The new leader not only has to come to terms with a new set of technicalities in placing runners, selecting anchors and finding the route but must also adjust to the increased exposure of the leader and the intimidating possibility of a long fall.

A number of strategies can be used to help the transition from second to leader:

---

1. Find a well-protected single-pitch climb that is comfortably within your abilities and get a more experienced companion to lead the climb and place protection. Follow the climb but leave the protection in place. Descend and then lead the climb yourself, clipping into the reliable pre-placed protection.
2. Select a similar climb and second it, but this time remove the protection placed by your leader. As you remove each piece look carefully at how it was placed. Descend and then lead the climb, placing your own protection.
3. Select a similar climb but this time lead it 'on sight' (without prior close inspection), placing as much protection as you can. Your placement of gear will be very much better if you have gone

79

through the kind of wet-day practice described in the previous chapter and the system will work best if you are with an encouraging and experienced companion. Finally, it is a good idea to pick a climb which is well within your abilities and one which is off the vertical so that you have time to think out what you are doing without running out of strength.

Runners

For the second, runners are quite useful in marking the line of the route and sometimes place the rope in a better position in the event of a slip, but generally they are a bit of a nuisance and tend to interrupt the flow of the ascent. For the leader, runners are invaluable and convert what might be an unjustifiably dangerous pitch into one that, with skill and imagination, can be climbed safely.

I have already explained the way in which runners operate (Chapter 3) and how to select and place anchors (Chapter 4). You might expect that

5.1 The leader has extended the runners to avoid rope drag before moving right.

placing runners is little different from placing anchors, but this is not really so. For a start, you are placing the runners as a pitch unrolls, so you are usually standing on relatively small holds and hanging on with one hand while you place the runner with the other. Sometimes, in situations such as laybacking or on overhanging rock, it is very difficult to take a hand off to place protection and you have to make a difficult choice between placing a runner and risking running out of strength, or pressing on while strength remains but risking a longer fall. The stances at the end of a pitch are usually on some sort of ledge system and you will often have a reasonable choice of places to construct anchors, but on a pitch you have to make do with what is available. Sometimes you will be spoilt for choice, but on climbs that have a reputation for poor protection you will have to use every bit of creativity to make the most of every possible placement. On a difficult and badly protected climb, a leader may spend 20 or 30 minutes fiddling with different choices of nuts or camming devices to get the best possible placement in an unpromising flared crack or awkwardly shaped pocket. The impatient will just press on but, in the event of a fall, the cautious climber who has invested time and energy in getting a half-decent runner (figure 5.1) will be in a very much better situation.

The spacing at which you place runners depends on how confident you are and what possibilities the rock offers. If you are climbing near your limit on a crack system that offers many opportunities for placing runners, you might place 20 or more runners on a 40m (130ft) pitch; if you are climbing well within your abilities you might only put three or four on the same pitch, whilst on a notoriously poorly protected pitch you might only get a single runner in 50m (165ft) of climbing.

Even if you are on relatively easy ground, I do not recommend totally abandoning the use of runners. It is very good practice for the leader to place a secure runner in the first few metres of a pitch since this converts a factor 2 fall direct onto the belayer (see Chapter 8) into one held through a runner, which greatly increases the chance of a fall being held. Also, there is always the possibility of a fall for reasons other than the sheer difficulty of the rock, particularly if the leader is hit by a falling stone or if a hold breaks.

Some years ago, I was climbing on a rarely visited crag in the Scottish Highlands on the second pitch of a climb of Very Severe standard. I had overcome the most difficult part, which passed a bulging overhang, and was on somewhat easier ground above but rather a long way above my last secure runner. I found a rather poor crack and spent a couple of minutes manoeuvring a small wedge into it. My sense of craftsmanship was offended by what was really a very poor placement and I shouted to my second that the runner was no use and that I would take it out and climb on. However, as sometimes happens, even though it was a poor placement it was not easily removed and so, as an afterthought, I clipped in the rope and moved upwards. About 3m (10ft) higher a large block of rock that I was climbing over levered out from the crag and both I and the block shot into space. I managed to push away the rock, which crashed harmlessly to the ground beneath, and I was held, after a fall of about 7m (23ft), on the runner that I had been trying to remove.

There are two lessons here: that sometimes falls happen when you are not expecting them and that even a poor runner is better than no runner at all. Without the runner that held me, I would have had a fall of about 20m (65ft) or more and would quite possibly have hit the rocks beneath.

There is tremendous craftsmanship in placing runners. If you watch someone climbing who is really competent, you will see them move up the rock, spot a placement for a runner and, almost without interrupting the flow of the ascent, select the right runner, place it and clip in the rope in a single, fluid movement. This is very efficient use of strength and maintains upward momentum. By contrast, a climber who is rusty will struggle to find the correct nut for the placement and will then fight to pull out rope to clip into the karabiner. This is tiring and takes the climber's concentration away from the climb.

Sometimes, runners help in breaking a pitch down into digestible fragments. A difficult pitch may be fiercely intimidating if you look at the whole 40m (135ft) or so but becomes a more reasonable proposition if you can break it down to 6m (20ft) to a resting point and a good runner, with another runner just above and so on.

Organizing equipment

Organizing or *racking* your equipment is an important ritual at the start of a pitch. It helps you to focus your concentration on the climb and, if you do it well, can greatly ease the selection of runners. Two main methods are available: to use bandoliers or to use loops on your harness.

Bandoliers are rather out of fashion, but I still like to use them. They are lengths of tape that pass diagonally across the chest and over the shoulder. They are often broader and padded in their upper part. Equipment is clipped to their narrower, lower section where it hangs at the climber's side without obstructing the view of feet and footholds.

Most modern harnesses come equipped with a number of short loops to which karabiners can be clipped. If your harness does not have this feature it is usually simple to improvise. Sometimes, on slab climbs, hardware on a bandolier tends to hang in your field of view. When that is the case, it is an easy matter to transfer it to the slings on your harness.

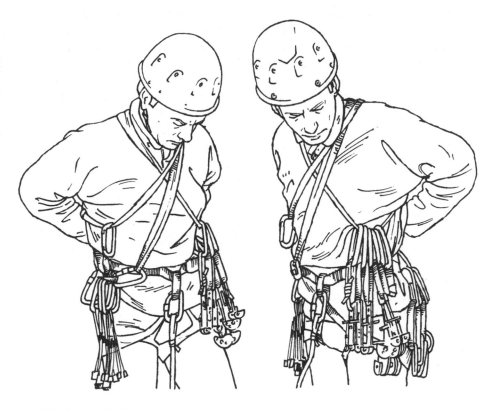

5.2 Gear racked ready for the pitch.

As you lead more and more climbs you will develop a racking system that suits you (figure 5.2). The aim is to be able to find and unclip a particular item quickly and easily. I carry small nuts on wire clipped in groups of three or four by size on a karabiner and I rack them on one bandolier with small ones at the front and large at the back and with all the karabiners in the same direction to aid unclipping. Further back on the same side are camming devices, again graded from small at the front to large at the back. Colour coding helps you to find exactly the right size once you are in roughly the right part of your rack. On the bandolier on my right-hand side I carry larger nuts on rope slings plus six or eight extenders (quick-draws) — short webbing slings about 8 or 10cm (3 or 4in) in length, each equipped with two karabiners. I have my tape slings draped over the left-hand shoulder and hanging down on the right side. I would normally carry three or four single-length tape slings and one or two double-length slings with screwgate karabiners and I always carry these in a way that allows me to remove them easily by unclipping one strand from the other. On the gear loops on my harness are my belay plate and some spare karabiners.

Everyone learns the hard way that time spent in organizing gear at the start of the pitch is an investment. Walk along the bottom of a popular crag and you will get the idea. I can guarantee there will be someone who is hanging on a move that is too difficult for them, desperately sorting through a tangle of hardware in a needle-in-the-haystack search for the right nut, or is going purple in the face both through frustration and from the tightening skein of slings that they are unsuccessfully trying to drag from round their neck.

You select your rack at the start of the climb in the light of what you expect the climb to involve. You will find little use for 10cm (4in) nuts on crackless slabs or for micronuts on most off-widths. On easier climbs it is normal to carry a smaller rack than on long and difficult ones. However, beware of leaving behind what might be a real life-saver. Climbs have a tremendous capacity to surprise and sometimes in the bowels of an awkward off-width you will find a tiny crack that will indeed take a welcome micronut or, in the middle of a crackless slab, a perfect pocket for a large camming device.

Keeping them in

One of climbing's more depressing experiences is to place a perfect runner after a difficult and poorly protected section and then, on moving up, to find that the runner drops out behind you. The time when runners are most likely to fall out is just as you move past them and you can prevent this by using a suitable extender to reduce the lifting effect of the rope. Sometimes it is worth moving past a vulnerable runner in a way that minimizes the outward pull exerted by the rope.

Some people seem to 'seat' every nut by jerking on it as though they are test-loading the breaking strain of the wire sling. This is not necessary. If a runner is not in danger of lifting out accidentally, as long as it is properly situated in the crack, it needs only a gentle pull to seat it. If, however, there is a substantial danger of the runner lifting, then do jerk it hard into its placement. Your second will not like this, since the nut will be hard to remove, but the leader's safety is normally considered to be more important than the second's convenience.

Sometimes spike runners tend to lift off and you can reduce this tendency by weighting the sling with some heavy pieces of surplus equipment or perhaps by wedging the knot in the crack behind the spike. (Incidentally, when all else fails, jammed knots are a surprisingly good alternative if you do not have the right sized nut for a crack.) Sometimes it is possible to place an upside-down nut either to resist the upward force on a belay or, in this context, to hold an important runner firmly in position against the tug of the rope.

Organizing the rope

If your rope runs in a zigzag manner through a number of runners it will produce a great deal of friction, which will impede your movement when leading the pitch and also tend to pull out all but the most secure runners. Sometimes, at the end of a long pitch, if you have not organized the rope correctly, you will find yourself having to pull rope through against the tremendous frictional drag before making each move. This is, at best, frustrating, and at worst dangerous, so it is much better to avoid it in the first place.

When climbing on a single rope this is achieved by extending runners (with long tape slings as well as quick-draws) or even omitting some that you do not judge to be crucial. One of the awkward situations to protect is when an easy traverse is followed by a direct upward ascent, such as when a ledge leads to the foot of a steep crack. If you place a runner at

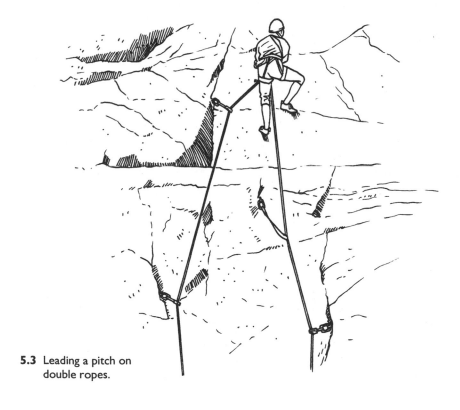

5.3 Leading a pitch on double ropes.

the foot of the crack it will tend to cause rope drag and will be prone to being lifted out by the rope so that your second, if slipping at the start of the traverse, will have a pendulum fall. The best solution depends on the exact circumstances, but using a long extension sling on the runner at the foot of the crack is probably the best of a number of rather unsatisfactory alternatives.

The use of double ropes (figures 5.3 and 8.2) permits the leader to use a complicated pattern of runners in an efficient way, allows one runner on each rope to be placed before a poorly protected section of a pitch, provides extra security in the event of one rope being damaged and, as has already been mentioned, increases the distance that can be abseiled. Against this are the disadvantages that double ropes are considerably more expensive, heavier to carry and, for the novice, rather more difficult to manage.

Judgement

The most common way for an experienced party to climb is by alternating leads with two climbers leap-frogging pitch after pitch. The leader on a particular pitch is the person who has to make most of the difficult decisions about route-finding and about how the pitch is to be managed. If you are the only leader on a long climb then, in effect, you are responsible for the entire enterprise. For a competent party climbing can be a wonderfully enjoyable and almost light-hearted affair, but you should never lose sight of the fact that things can, and do, go wrong and that circumstances can magnify apparently trivial errors into major catastrophes. It is all too easy on a delightful, sunny day to neglect the careful management of the rope or the selection of sound anchors, but in the oft-quoted words of Edward Whymper, after the first ascent of the Matterhorn ended in tragedy,

> Climb if you will, but remember that courage and strength are nought without prudence and that a momentary negligence may destroy the happiness of a lifetime. Do nothing in haste, look well to each step and from the beginning think what may be the end.

Abseiling

Beginners love abseiling (figure 5.4). It is exciting, spectacular and – once you have built up your confidence – relatively easy. You may find it strange that abseiling appears so late in this book, but its positioning is deliberate. Abseiling is one of the most potentially hazardous activities that climbers undertake and there is a depressing catalogue of outstandingly good climbers who have been killed as a result of abseiling accidents.

Abseiling or *rappelling* is a method of making a controlled descent down a crag by using friction from the rope to slow your descent. The friction can be created either by wrapping the rope around the body in a certain way or by using a friction brake such as a belay plate on the harness. It is often practised as a fun activity for beginners, but its real use in climbing is to descend ground too steep to be conveniently climbed down, such as in approaching the base of a sea cliff, or to retreat from a climb in the event of bad weather. It is widely used in alpine climbing to facilitate the descent from long climbs where 20 or 30 consecutive abseils may be needed.

Normally, abseiling takes place on a double rope and at the foot of the abseil the rope can then be retrieved by pulling on one of the two strands.

Basic techniques
Classic abseil
The so-called classic abseil, where the rope is wrapped around the body, is rarely used except, for instance, in a hill-walking emergency where someone might be carrying a light rope but no climbing equipment. A modification of the classic abseil is to use the rope through a karabiner clipped to the front of the harness and over the shoulder. Both of these methods are rather uncomfortable and cause quite considerable wear and tear on clothing or, if you are wearing light clothes, your body.

Belay plate method
The method that I recommend is to use your belay plate attached with a screwgate karabiner to the strong point at the front of your harness. This attachment point should be high so that you are not top-heavy when abseiling. The abseil rope passes through the belay device and the screwgate karabiner, and the control ropes (there would normally be two) are controlled by the abseiler. To allow this method to be used, you need a model of belay plate that has two slots or that permits two ropes to be used simultaneously.

Descenders
If you expect to do lots of abseiling you might invest in a purpose-made device such as a figure-of-eight descender (figure 5.4). This is slightly more convenient to use than a belay plate and usually has slightly better heat absorption so it does not become so hot in use, but I find that I very rarely use a descender and manage perfectly well with my belay plate.

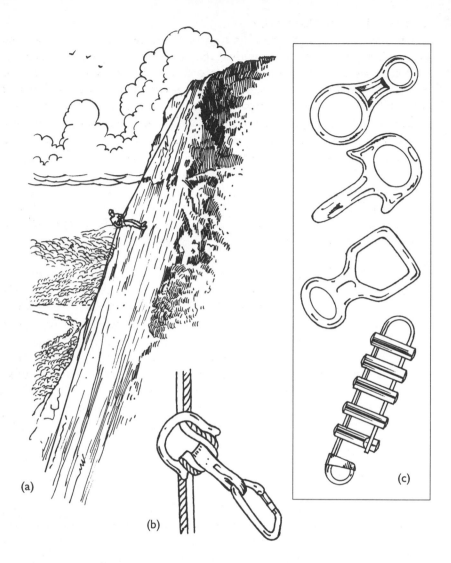

5.4 Abseiling: (a) general view; (b) brake in use; (c) descenders.

Munter hitch

The final method would be to use a Munter hitch (see Chapter 4). This works well but is inclined to twist the rope rather badly. It is a useful method if you are unfortunate enough to drop your belay plate but you must ensure that the direction of movement of the rope is such that it tends to tighten the screwgate rather than loosen it!

Controlling the dead rope

When abseiling, it is vital to keep control of the dead rope as it enters the belay plate. If you are not confident that you are getting enough friction, you can use both hands on this rope or even take the rope around your back and give it a twist around the opposite wrist rather in the manner of a body belay. I recommend that you become familiar in a well-controlled situation with the degree of friction that your particular system provides. Remember that different belay plates and friction devices provide differing degrees of friction as do different diameters and makes of climbing rope.

Making the descent

You should keep your body well out from the rock so that your feet tend to push onto the rock. If you are in too upright a position, your feet will constantly slip. Avoid jerking the abseil rope and try to progress smoothly and in control.

If you have to stop for some time part way down an abseil, you can hold your position by carefully wrapping three turns of the control rope around your thigh. It is then possible to take off your hands, for instance, to remove a stubborn runner left on the pitch. It is worth keeping your feet about 50cm (20in) apart in order to increase your lateral stability but generally, once started, abseils progress smoothly. If possible, it is worth selecting a high anchor point otherwise there can be a very awkward manoeuvre to get over the edge of the crag.

If the rock overhangs, you will lose contact with it and hang free. This is less of a problem than you might expect and with a good sit-harness you can sit quite comfortably and continue your descent.

Abseiling for real
Anchors

When climbers abseil for real, it is one of the few times in climbing when they are entirely dependent on the security of the anchor that they choose. If you have attached the abseil rope to a sling over a poor spike or have placed a less than perfect nut and the anchor fails, it will do so when your entire weight is on the rope. You have no further support and will probably fall to oblivion. I cannot overemphasize how important it is to abseil only on anchors in which you have total confidence. In a real abseil situation you will probably have to abandon equipment and it is hard to persuade yourself to leave two pieces of gear when you think that one might suffice. Just imagine that fraction of a second after the anchor has failed and your view of whether the money saved was worthwhile.

Sometimes a single anchor – like a large tree or a well-formed and entirely secure spike – will suffice. In order to help retrieval of the rope afterwards, you should use a sling to attach the abseil rope. This is not strictly necessary on trees, but be aware that the repeated retrieval of abseil ropes can damage the bark of trees and thus threaten their health and strength.

If you are in any doubt about the security of your anchor, then add a second one and try to link them together with a sling or length of tape so that they are equally loaded by the weight of the abseiling climber. If you are climbing on double ropes, pass one strand through the sling and join both ropes with a double fisherman's knot. With a single rope, thread one end through the sling until you reach the half-way point of the rope. Starting from the sling, work down the doubled rope to ensure that it is running freely and hand-coil the last 20m (65ft) or so. Shout, 'Below,' and throw the hand-coils out from the rock. For a single rope, position the centre mark at the sling and follow a similar procedure. The rope is now ready for the first abseiler to descend.

Making the descent
It is sound practice for the heaviest member of the party to descend first with an additional but non-load-bearing back-up anchor clipped into the system. When that climber is safely at the foot of the abseil the additional back-up is then removed – the system has now been tested. Before the last person descends it is checked that the rope will run for retrieval and confirmed which of the two ropes is to be pulled (hopefully, they are of different colours). On arrival at the foot of the abseil, the first climber constructs an anchor for his or her own security and clips in. The second climber, when joining the first, is also secured and then one strand of the rope is pulled to retrieve the rope.

Rope jams
If the rope jams, try to flick it and reposition yourself for a pull from a slightly different direction. If all this fails, you have a serious problem. If you still have both strands of the rope then, in principle, it is possible to secure yourself with a prusik loop (Chapter 8) whilst climbing the double ropes. If the joining knot has reached you, then you will have one rope with which to attempt to climb back up to the anchor point, but this may well be impossible.

The end
Finally, you should note that people have on more than one occasion abseiled off the end of their ropes. It is possible to guard against this by tying a knot in the ends of the rope but this does present its own difficulties in that if the abseil ropes are blown into an undesirable position the knot can prevent their retrieval.

6

The crag environment

Environment

We were half-way up a long and beautiful climb on Binnein Shuas, a remote Highland crag. I was leading the third pitch and about 30m (100ft) above my second when I heard the peculiar whirring, rumbling noise that sometimes comes with stonefall. Instinctively I leant into the rock and protected my head, but on hearing the sound pass well out from me I turned, just in time to see a stooping peregrine falcon striking its prey, an unfortunate small bird which exploded in a cloud of feathers. Even lowland crags have a scent of wildness about them, but crags found in wild mountains or on rugged sea cliffs can present true wilderness in which we should tread with respect. When you start to climb, particularly if you start on a climbing wall or a crag in an urban situation it is easy to be so absorbed in the technicalities as to ignore the wider crag environment. Encounters such as the one with the peregrine falcon are a great privilege, but one that we must defend, for if climbers were to go there during the nesting season the peregrines are unlikely to nest successfully.

On another occasion, I was descending unroped down steep but easy rock to the base of a sea cliff when I had a strong sensation that I was not alone. I glanced between my feet and, bobbing up and down in the water 6m (20ft) below me, was the all-too-human face of an Atlantic grey seal. There was a long moment of recognition between two not-so-distant species and then the seal turned, effortlessly rejoining its own medium – the deep green ocean.

The first recorded explorations of British mountain crags came from nineteenth-century botanists in pursuit of arctic alpine rarities. The steep and clean faces frequented by modern climbers do not harbour very much vegetation, but if you climb on some of the less frequented chimney or gully climbs you may still find a rich flora. These plants have been there for thousands of years and the least that climbers can do is to try to co-exist with them and not reduce every piece of rock to a climbing-wall-like state of sterility.

Ethics

Climbing owes much of its existence and attraction to codes of tradition and ethics hallowed by time. The style of an ascent is all. It is usually possible to get to the top of any crag by a route considerably less difficult than the one on which you are climbing – hence the emphasis on style and not just on reaching the top. Climbers talk of 'pure' and 'clean' ascents and each area will have its own rules. You will absorb the ethics of your own climbing area and your own climbing contemporaries, but if you climb elsewhere try not to offend the locals!

Sandstone and chalk

The most elaborately codified climbing practices that I have encountered have been on the tremendous sandstone towers of Bohemia and this has probably arisen both from its isolation from mainstream climbing and a period of economic deprivation. To protect the rock, metal nuts were taboo and the leader had to be skilful in the use of jammed knots. Often these would not be possible and the climber had to rely on very widely spaced iron bolts inserted in the rock. Chalk was not used and the footwear of the person that I climbed with appeared to be cut-down football boots with thin soles of soft rubber. These rules may be arbitrary but they seem to have protected the spirit and the excitement of climbing in that area so that you can still enjoy the same climbs in more or less the same way as the pioneers 50 years ago.

Chalk is contentious. Although it does make life for the leader some-what easier, its adverse effects include an unsightly trail of white marks delineating a climb. Sometimes, on popular routes, the appropriate holds are liberally coated in chalk and the climber no longer has the fascinating exercise of deciding which set of holds to use – it is reduced to a kind of climbing by numbers.

Bolts and pitons

Central to the ethics of most climbing areas is that the minimum force should be used to make an ascent. Therefore, if a climb has been ascended 'clean' (that is, without the use of direct assistance from placed equipment) then an ascent that utilizes such aid is judged inferior.

This is a matter for the individual climber except when the placement of pitons or bolts or the chipping of holds adversely affects the climb for subsequent parties. Some beautiful cracks have been permanently scarred by the damaging effect of pitons or are disfigured with rusting lumps of metal, although in fairness it should be pointed out that many clean ascents are only possible because piton scars have made perfect pockets for finger jams and modern nut protection.

The use of bolts is one of the big issues in modern climbing. Their supporters will argue that expansion bolts in holes drilled in the rock provide protection which allows climbing to take place on huge areas of rock that were previously inaccessible to climbers. Their use is widespread in southern Europe on steep limestone crags and they do provide superb climbing which is exciting without really being dangerous. The opponents of bolts argue that bolts have removed the word 'impossible' from the climber's vocabulary and that the tremendously bold leads that climbers might make in 20 or 30 years' time are being desecrated by bolts which 'bring the climb down' to the standard of current climbers.

Personally, I have enjoyed climbing on bolt-protected routes and have been grateful for the occasional bolt ladder rendering some of the big Californian walls feasible, but I would be horrified to see some of our great traditional crags, steeped in history, being subjected to assaults by teams of rock athletes with electric drills.

Etiquette

Relax, this is *not* about extending your little finger when you are drinking tea! Quite simply, the biggest impact that many climbers have is on other crag users. Whilst I swerve from giving you a lecture on how to behave, litter (trash), excessive noise, hogging routes so that your equipment is in place and prevents anyone else gaining access, kicking off loose stones and defecating on ledges are all activities guaranteed to ruin someone else's day.

Solo climbing

Climbing without ropes or companions is undoubtedly the purest form, though its risks are evident. There is a joy in moving in this way that some people find irresistible, but it is not for everyone. The smallest mistake can have disastrous consequences. Some astonishing ascents have been made by solo climbers such as Peter Croft and Jimmy Jewell, but you also see climbers who are clearly out of their depth radiating anxiety to adjacent roped parties. If someone is determined to climb solo, doing so on the same climbs as roped parties seems to be rather perverse.

Weather

Having looked at the effect that climbers themselves can have on the crag environment and on other climbers, it is now time to look at the main external factor that affects your day's climbing – the weather.

Weather has a powerful effect both on crags and on climbers. Each winter wreaks subtle changes to the rock, levering off a small flake here, loosening a boulder there, but most of this happens when the crag is unfrequented and the most obvious effects of weather are felt more directly.

Rain

Rain has a dramatic effect on most climbs and increases the standard of difficulty enormously. If you commonly climb at Very Severe standard in the British grading system, you will find that in wet conditions many Difficult and Very Difficult climbs are at least as difficult as Very Severes in the dry. Rain breaks down the friction between boot and rock and also, to a lesser extent, that of hand on footholds. If the crag is covered in lichen, a film of water converts it to a surface like a skating rink in a matter of minutes.

Few people deliberately climb in such conditions but once you have made the effort to go out, you can have a very entertaining day if you choose a climb that is much easier than your normal standard. Do not underestimate the difficulties that you are likely to meet, for a simple move on sloping holds that you would barely notice in dry conditions can become a formidable obstacle. If possible, choose a climb with relatively sharp-edged and positive holds rather than a friction slab, and it is also worth trying to climb in heavyweight walking or climbing boots with cleated soles. A useful dodge is to climb with old socks over your rock boots since this greatly improves their adhesion on wet rock. Incidentally, a side effect of climbing on wet rock is that your hands become very soft and much more prone to cuts and abrasions from the rocks. This can be a serious problem on multi-day climbs, even in dry conditions, and climbers will often guard against this by taping their finger ends and knuckles.

If the rain starts while you are on a long climb, you have a number of choices, none of which are particularly attractive. They include sitting it out, abandoning the attempt or forcing an ascent.

Sitting it out

You can sit out the rain keeping your fingers crossed and hoping that it is a passing shower. On clean, south-facing cliffs the rock will dry out very rapidly after rain if there is any trace of sun and wind. However, lichenous, north-facing crags are likely to take several days to recover.

Abandoning the climb

You can abandon the attempt and descend. If the climb is one of some difficulty, you are unlikely to be able to *down-climb* in the wet and so your descent is likely to be by abseil. Be alert to the fact that heavy rain is likely to affect your concentration during the descent and you should guard carefully to prevent this from happening. Your rope is likely to become saturated with water and as you abseil your friction device will neatly squeeze most of this over your legs.

Forcing an ascent

You can force an ascent. Although you would not claim it as a normal ascent, it is sometimes better to escape upwards than downwards. Generally, this would consist of using every form of assistance at your disposal to complete the climb. It is worth trying to climb, perhaps with socks over your boots, with the frequent placing of runners to assess how feasible the ascent will be. It is unlikely that this will succeed for the whole climb and you may either have to find an easier route, perhaps where your route and a less difficult one cross, or use direct aid from runners.

At its simplest, this involves using runners as handholds, but when this becomes too strenuous it is worth standing in single-length tape slings clipped into the runners on difficult sections. The most common mistake is to make these slings too long. The best approach is to place the sling so that you can just get your foot into it after raising your leg in a kind of cancan manoeuvre. From there you can strenuously stand up, but in so doing gain a reasonable amount of height which, after all, is the object of the exercise. Do not forget, in your enthusiasm to pull on your runners, to clip the rope into some of them for protection.

I have painful memories of an autumn day in Glen Etive in Scotland when we made more than our fair share of mistakes. We started rather late in the day on a climb of about 250m (820ft). It had been wet all week, but as we started to climb the crag appeared to have dried out. Unfortunately, all the cracks were still weeping water and this made the climbing both slow and difficult. We decided to press on regardless but near the top of the climb a steep, overhanging corner had us resorting to all-out aid climbing techniques in the gathering gloom. By this time, it had started to rain again. We, of course, had no waterproofs with us and arrived at the top of the crag in pitch darkness, shivering cold, soaking wet and with a very difficult descent ahead of us. One of the odd things about climbing is that the intense memories of that sort of day are remarkably satisfying (in retrospect!) and linger long after the recollections of warm, sunny days have passed!

Loss of body heat

I have mentioned that climbing in the wet is very slow. It is also very strenuous and tiring. If you are on a long climb and conditions are cold, you can find yourself in a dangerous situation as heat drains from your body to a point where your performance starts to be affected. If you are on a long climb and the weather is unsettled, it is worth carrying a light waterproof and perhaps a fleece jacket with you. If these are put in a light rucksack, the second can carry it without undue difficulty and it will greatly strengthen your position should the weather break.

There is a vogue in the Alps and elsewhere for very rapid ascents of long rock climbs. People often go on climbs of perhaps 1000m (3300ft) with little more than the clothing and equipment they would use on a roadside crag. This is wonderfully lightweight climbing when things are going well, but should a storm break – and unpredicted storms are common in high mountains – then you are extremely vulnerable.

A few years ago two very experienced climbers who had chosen to make a rapid ascent of the North Face of the Piz Badile (a classic rock climb in Switzerland) succumbed to the cold of a sudden storm and perished.

Snow

Sometimes if you are climbing in a high mountain area, it is inevitable that it will start to snow. In cold, dry conditions this can sometimes leave the rock dry and you can climb reasonably successfully as long as you keep your fingers warm – perhaps by using thin gloves or fingerless mitts ('miser mitts'). Normally, however, the rock will become wet and, of course, the lower ambient temperatures increase the problems unless you are very well clad.

Heat

Excessive heat is rarely a problem in Britain but is more common in Australia, California and southern Europe. You will find it very hard to concentrate if you are too hot, so get round the problem by choosing to climb on north-facing cliffs during the heat of the day, or make an early start and then take a long siesta before resuming climbing in the cool of the evening. On a long climb, you should carry water with you and take care that you do not become dehydrated. Becoming seriously overheated (heatstroke) is an extremely dangerous condition and we will look at this in the first aid section of this chapter (see page 101).

Weather forecasts

Weather forecasts are useful as long as you take care to translate them according to the conditions that will prevail on the crag. If you are in a mountain area, winds will be higher and temperatures generally lower than those forecast for low ground. There will also be an increased likelihood of cloud cover and increased precipitation. If you are climbing away from regular weather forecasts, then regular inspection of the sky can give many clues as can the carrying of a pocket altimeter or a barometric watch.

At its simplest:

- A rising atmospheric pressure is a generally favourable sign.
- A decreasing atmospheric pressure spells a message of probable bad weather.
- A steady barometric pressure suggests little immediate change.
- Rapidly changing pressure should lead you to expect high winds.

Meteorologists will probably be horrified at this over-simplification, but if you are guided by this and regularly compare atmospheric pressure with the weather around you, you will quickly learn to predict with a good degree of accuracy.

Be aware that changing altitude also affects pressure and allow for this by readjusting your altimeter at any known spot-height.

Adverse conditions

Weather is the main source of these but others exist.

Earthquakes and stonefalls

Recently climbers in California were horrified to experience an earthquake during which they could feel the cracks flexing and changing in width. More mundane but more dangerous is the risk of stonefall. As has already been mentioned, this is commonly caused by other climbers, but also by the sun's loosening ice-cemented stones on alpine climbs during the heat of the day. There is no safe approach if stonefall is prevalent. Start early to avoid the heat of the day and keep away from gullies and chimney systems that tend to funnel stones. If you must cross such an area, cross it rapidly, be vigilant and be grateful if you are wearing a helmet.

Sea cliffs

Sea cliffs provide their own hazards and more than one heavily laden climber has drowned in a so-called 'freak' wave. Most people believe that waves are regular in size. They are not, and if you watch a set of waves for long enough a particularly large one will come along. If this arrives when you are standing unroped at the foot of a sea cliff you can be washed away with little chance of being able to swim.

Insects

In warmer climes, snakes and swarms of bees can detract seriously from the enjoyment of a climb, but of course none of these are as ferocious as the Scottish midge. I was once climbing on the Etive Slabs on a moist

August day when the fresh breeze that had kept the midges away all day suddenly dropped. All across the crag, parties could be seen rushing to set up abseils. One or two unfortunate leaders high on unprotected pitches, desperately tried to maintain maximum contact with the rock whilst simultaneously yelling for top ropes and scraping the carnivorous midges off their faces.

Navigation

Some guide books have very detailed descriptions as to how to find a cliff, with three-dimensional sketches of the approach terrain. Others unhelpfully assume that anyone who is not totally incompetent will obviously know where the crag is situated. If you are new to an area it is almost always worth investing in a map of 1:25 000 or 1:50 000 scale and many guide books recommend particular sheets of the map.

This a book about climbing and not about navigation, but if you are climbing on crags away from the road, you do need to master a few basic techniques.

Navigation techniques:

- Setting the map or orientating it to the landscape.
- Lifting a bearing from the map.
- Walking on a bearing.
- Identifying the major features by their contour pattern. These would be ridges, cwms or coires, cols, summits and valleys.
- Using timing to estimate distance.
- Recognizing the conventional signs marking craggy ground, water features such as marshy ground and footpaths. Many beginners have been disappointed to find that what they had interpreted as a promising footpath was, in fact, a parish boundary with no visible marking or assistance on the ground.

To use some of these techniques you require a compass – the type that combines a compass and a protractor is probably the simplest to use. The *Outward Bound Map and Compass Handbook* or a similar book will give you the grounding that you require in these techniques.

Route-finding

Navigation in rocky terrain makes greater demands than it would in the low country. Usually what is required is a combination of navigation and route-finding. Route-finding is a difficult skill to acquire and is best learnt if you apply careful concentration to finding the best route through a complex area of broken, craggy ground. After a while, you will get the hang of linking together ramps, ledge systems and lines of weakness, but until you are fully confident, take care that you can always retrace your steps.

Rock climbers have often come to grief during the descent from a climb. This is usually down 'easier' ground to the side of the cliff, but such descents can often be very tricky. Before starting a climb, always check with the guide book to make sure that you know how to descend. This is also the time to do a visual reconnaissance of the way down. Often, the obvious way is not the best.

Once, while still at school, my friend and I were delighted to succeed in a long and difficult climb on a Welsh mountain crag. We had given no thought to the descent in our eagerness to climb and so rushed off down the obvious feature. Some hours later, two chastened young climbers at last read the descent section of the guide book: 'East gully is not recommended as a descent. It is dangerously loose, vegetated and treacherous.' We could only agree!

When route-finding on broken ground it is common to look upwards and see the rocky outcrops clearly but not the ledges. This means that things often (but not always) look steeper and more difficult than they actually are. Conversely, when looking down your eye picks up the ledges and misses the intervening crags, so things look much easier than they really are. This can be extremely dangerous and only experience will allow you to judge how difficult such ground is going to be. If in doubt, retrace your steps and try elsewhere. Usually, by traversing you will eventually reach relatively easy ground.

Mountain safety

Safety in the mountains is largely an attitude of mind. You are much more likely to be well-prepared if you take the problem seriously and make a sensible assessment of what the risks might be. A broken ankle may be a relatively simple problem if it occurs in a car park. The situation is much more difficult if you are half an hour's walk over rough ground from help and the problem is a very serious one if you are several days' able-bodied walk from assistance.

The best recipe for mountain safety is to keep asking 'What if?' and to equip yourself for a moderately pessimistic scenario. I have sometimes met groups from the armed services who come to climbing areas equipped with stretchers and large first aid rucksacks. This is clearly safe, but it does mean that there is additional equipment and tends to detract from the spontaneity of the day.

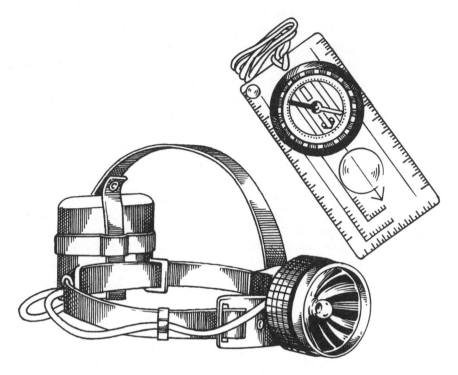

6.1 Compass and headtorch.

I would suggest that your mountain safety checklist is as follows:

- Proper clothing to deal with changes in weather conditions.
- Survival bag.
- Emergency rations.
- Map and compass.
- First aid kit.
- Helmet.
- Torch
- Dark glasses, sun block, insect repellent.

Obviously if you are climbing five minutes' walk from your car you hardly need a survival bag or, indeed, several of the other items. If, however, you are caught out in the wilds by darkness or bad weather, one of the strong but lightweight polythene bivi sacks and a couple of chocolate bars can be lifesavers.

First aid

I do not believe that rock climbing is any more dangerous than driving a car but, as in that activity, accidents do occur. Someone once said to me that mountain accidents either require sticking plaster or a shovel, and whilst this is rather extreme, the idea is appropriate. It is useful to have small pieces of sticking plaster, minor headache remedies and so on, but you should really be equipped for the life-threatening injuries that might, if you are very unlucky, occur to someone climbing nearby.

Also, before going out it is important to know who coordinates the rescue services in your area so that a group going for help can dial the appropriate emergency number. In the UK, for example, you should dial 999 and ask for the police, who call out and coordinate rescues, although the teams are actually unpaid amateurs. In the USA, the ranger service often both controls and forms the rescue team and in Europe, professional mountain guides carry out rescues. While rescues in the UK are free, other countries (including other European countries and the USA) charge for the rescue services. (Check that your insurance gives you ample cover to pay for a call-out, before you need to do so.)

No responsible person should head for the great outdoors until they have been on a recognized first aid training course. The Red Cross, the St John Ambulance and the St Andrew's Ambulance Association all run excellent courses and the telephone number of your nearest local branch can be found in the telephone directory. Many of the key techniques used in first aid – especially mouth-to-mouth ventilation and chest compression cannot be learned from books and must be practised under the supervision of a qualified trainer. Books, including this one and the more detailed *Outward Bound First Aid Handbook*, should be regarded as reference works rather than as substitutes for training.

Often the best emergency first aid action is to do nothing at all, other than minimize the danger to the patient and seek qualified help at once. You can do a great deal of harm by over-enthusiastic medical treatment. For this reason, this section deals with lifesaving procedures and the treatment of minor ailments but it does not go into in-depth diagnosis, or procedures such as tensioning broken limbs.

The emphasis in your first aid should be to:

- Preserve the life of the victim.
- Prevent any further harm or deterioration.
- Send promptly for qualified help.
- Promote recovery, if within your means.

The order in which you should carry out first aid procedures is:

1. Safety.
2. Body check.
3. Cardiopulmonary resuscitation (CPR).
4. Bleeding.
5. Burns.
6. Shock and hypothermia.
7. Other injuries and conditions.

Safety

Your first thought when approaching any victim is to make the accident area safe for yourself and other people. For example: if the accident is the result of stonefall, be alert to the possibility of further danger from falling rock and position yourself and others accordingly.

Never move a patient with a spinal injury, except as a last resort. If it is essential that the victim be moved at once (because of the danger of falling rocks, for example) great care must be taken, especially if it looks as though the victim has a damaged neck or spine. Quick indicators of a possible spinal injury are the nature of the accident, the position in which the victim is lying, and the lack of any sensation in the limbs.

When turning or lifting a victim with a suspected spinal injury:

- Use at least three or four people acting together.
- Move head, trunk and legs together, keeping the head supported.
- Avoid any rotation or bending of the spine.

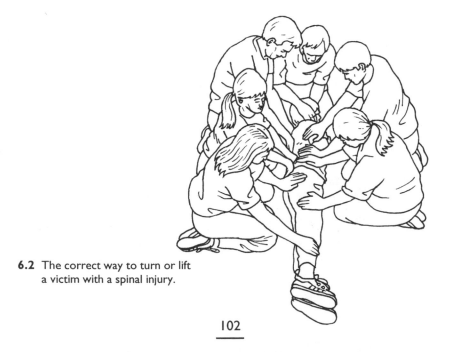

6.2 The correct way to turn or lift a victim with a spinal injury.

A victim who needs to be moved can be rolled (as shown in figure 6.3) onto a stretcher or board (if available). Moving a spinal victim is best left to experts, and unless there is a very immediate risk to life and limb, it is better not to attempt this at all.

Assessing the casualty

The next step is to perform a body check to ascertain the actual damage. To a large extent this is the most important element of first aid. The very first question you need to ask is whether the patient is conscious or not. If more than one patient is injured, always attend to the unconscious ones first; your priority being to see that they can breathe.

Remember your priorities by the maxim
Airway, Breathing, Circulation (ABC):

- Airway
  If the casualty is unconscious check that the airway is clear. Noisy breathing is an indication that the airway is blocked. Remove from the mouth any obstruction, such as loose dentures or mud. Tilt the head back by gently lifting the chin; this will clear the tongue from the back of the throat and open the airway.
- Breathing
  Place your ear near the victim's mouth. Can you hear breathing or feel any breath on your cheek? While doing this, place your hand gently on the abdomen and look along the body. Can you feel the abdomen rising and falling, or see the chest doing the same?
- Circulation
  At the same time, feel for the victim's pulse by placing your finger-tips (not thumb) on the neck, just behind the Adam's apple, in the gap between the windpipe and the muscle alongside it.

If the three ABC checks show a problem with the breathing or circulation then you need to take immediate action. If you cannot detect a pulse, waste no time in seeking help. Get to the nearest telephone and call an ambulance, leaving the patient alone if necessary (this is the *only* occasion on which you should consider leaving the patient alone). On returning to the patient, give mouth-to-mouth ventilation and chest compression until help arrives (these lifesaving techniques are designed to maintain the oxygen supply to the brain until the medical team arrives). To learn how to use these resuscitation techniques, you should attend a first aid course.

The body check

If the victim is fully conscious, and there are no problems with the ABC checks, continue with the body check. This is simply a case of working down the body and looking for signs of injuries. While doing so you should talk to the casualty (do this even if they are unconscious; they may be much more aware than you think). Reassure them, explain what you are doing and ask them to tell you if anything you do hurts them. Watch their face to see if the expression changes as you touch parts of the body.

Ask for the history of the accident if you did not see it, and ask whether anyone else was involved (there may be another victim lying unconscious nearby). Always remember that the obvious injury may not be the life-threatening one.

Head

Always start at the head. Look for any obvious injury and check for blood or fluid coming from the ears or nose which might indicate damage inside the skull. Check the eyes for foreign bodies or damage and the pupils for comparative size and reaction to light (which might indicate concussion). Feel if the skin is hot, cold, clammy or dry. These, together with other signs, could suggest hypothermia, heatstroke and/or shock. Finally be aware of the breathing: is it fast or slow, deep or shallow, and is it regular or struggling?

Neck

Move down to the neck and feel around for any obvious injury or dampness from bleeding. Check to see if the casualty is wearing a warning medallion such as those worn by diabetics or epileptics. Be aware of the pulse rate.

Trunk

Working on both sides of the trunk, press the ribs in carefully to see if there is a reaction by the victim which would indicate a chest or rib injury. Feel for abnormal hardness in the abdomen. Feel under the back for obvious injury, deformity or dampness from bleeding.

Limbs

Work along the arms and then the legs, feeling for any unusual limb position, swelling, or bleeding. Check for a warning bracelet indicating diabetes, epilepsy, etc. See if the casualty can move the arms, legs, fingers and toes. If not, ask where the pain or difficulty lie.

Diagnosis

This body check only takes a few minutes, but it could be a lifesaver. Having made the check you are in a better position to inform the rescue services of the likely nature of the problem, so that they can gauge the level of their response.

The recovery position

Once the initial checks have been completed, an unconscious victim needs to be placed in the recovery position – unless suffering from a spinal injury (see page 102) – to prevent them choking on their own vomit or ingesting the acids produced by the stomach (see figure 6.3).

Kneeling beside the casualty, straighten the legs. Place the arm nearest to you at right angles to the casualty's body, then bend the upper arm parallel with the body, with the palm facing up. All the time ensure that the head is kept tilted back and the airway clear. Bring the arm furthest away from you across the casualty's chest and place their hand against the cheek nearest to you, with the palm facing outwards. This will cushion the patient's face and head when they are rolled over. Using your other hand, hold the thigh furthest from you and, keeping the casualty's foot flat on the floor, draw up the knee. Keeping the casualty's hand pressed against their cheek, pull the raised thigh towards you. This will roll the casualty neatly into the correct recovery position.

Ensure that the head is kept tilted back and supported on the casualty's hand. Once in this position the casualty should never be left alone but should be closely monitored for breathing problems or the state of their consciousness.

Getting help

Prompt action on the part of trained medics is the key to preventing the loss of life in emergencies. Ideally you should choose two competent members of your party to summon help, while the remainder stay with the casualty. Of course, if there are only two of you, the decision whether to stay with or leave the patient is extremely difficult, and will depend on factors such as the weather, how far you are from habitation and the nature of the patient's injuries. If you stay with the patient, you can use a whistle or torch to attract attention. (Six long blasts or flashes are the internationally recognized distress calls; these are answered with three short blasts or flashes).

Make sure that those who go to summon help know the patient's precise location. If you are unsure of the grid reference, you can at least make a note of prominent landmarks in the area and take compass bearings from them to find your approximate position.

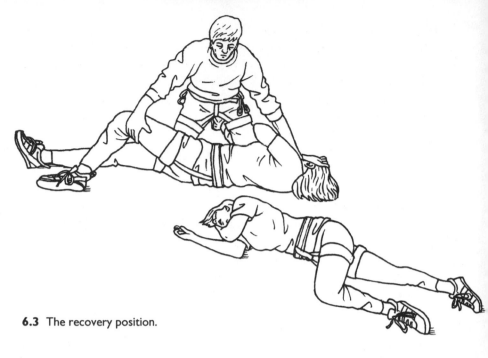

6.3 The recovery position.

A rescue team can be told the blood group and height in millimetres of a casualty, but they can do little to help if they do not know where the incident is. Marking a map and sending this as part of the message is helpful as are a grid reference, compass bearings from prominent objects and the name of the climb and crag on which the incident took place. Thus, a good message would be: 'John Smith, aged 47, fell onto ledge at foot of pitch 3, Sledgate Ridge, Gable Crag, grid reference 213105. Compound fracture of right lower leg. No other visible injuries. Patient conscious and in good spirits. Accompanied by William Wilson, aged 34, fit and a competent first aider. The casualty has no known medical conditions. Time of accident approximately 1450, weather cool but dry.'

Be prepared to give the following information to the rescue services:

- Numbers and names of casualties.
- Precise location.
- Your assessment of the nature of their injuries.
- The age, condition and state of mind of the casualties.
- The time of the accident and the weather conditions at the scene.

Most accidents follow someone hitting the ground or a ledge. Occasionally, an injured climber will be suspended from the rope and this can make rescue extremely difficult. Unless very experienced, the party in the field can do little other than endeavour to lower the injured climber to a more comfortable or more approachable position. Rescuing an injured climber half-way up a large crag may involve dozens of rescuers, ropes up to 300m (980ft) in length and the use of a great deal of specialized equipment, including helicopters. It is much better not to have the accident in the first place!

Specific procedures

Once you have sent for help you can begin to treat the patient's injuries.

Bleeding

Blood loss should be attended to rapidly. Internal bleeding is revealed by a number of signs, which may include bruising, discolouring and/or bleeding from the body openings. There is little you can do to treat internal bleeding except for treating the shock that will almost certainly accompany it (see page 108).

The treating of external bleeding is more straightforward. Remember two things: elevation and direct pressure. Elevating the wound will help to slow the rate of blood flow. Direct pressure can be applied to the wound with anything available. In the case of major bleeding, hygiene comes a low second so do not be afraid to use your hand tight against the wound or use a dirty rag, if that is all that is available; any risk of infection can be worried about later.

Get a dressing on the wound straightaway, but do not bind the wound too tightly; your aim is to stop the bleeding, not cut off the blood supply to the limbs. If blood starts to seep through the first dressing, place another dressing directly on top of it. Do not remove the first dressing.

Burns

There is only one first aid treatment for burns, no matter what the severity: the whole wound should be immersed in cold, preferably running, water. Remove anything that is in the way of the burn (clothing, rings, watches and so on) but never try to remove anything that is actually sticking to the burn, such as clothing. The wound area should be left in the water for at least ten minutes, and considerably longer for anything more than a very minor burn. Do not stop treatment just because the wound stops hurting; keep it in the water for a good few minutes after that. Prompt treatment of even a serious burn will have dramatic beneficial effects.

Never apply lotions, ointments or creams to any burn. One of the worst misapprehensions in first aid is that fat (such as butter or margarine) cools a burn. This may be the initial effect but the longer term effect is that the wound literally cooks in the fat.

If the skin on the burn is not broken, it should be left open to the air. If the skin is blistered or broken, use a clean, light dressing made of non-fluffy material to cover the wound and keep out infection. Plastic kitchen film makes an ideal burns dressing, or you could use a clean plastic bag.

Scalds, caused by hot liquids, should be treated in the same way. Treat any burns victims for shock (see below) and keep a close check that the airway does not become obstructed while the patient is lying down to recover.

Sunburn

Prevention is far better than cure for this condition, so wear protective clothing and use sun blocks on exposed and vulnerable areas, such as the back of the neck, the face and lips, and the feet. After-sun lotions and calamine lotion will help to relieve minor burning.

Shock and hypothermia

These conditions can be killers in their own right. They can also be the underlying (and more serious) problem in an accident. In both instances, the first safeguard is protection from the elements. Survival bags (large heavyweight plastic bags) can be used as emergency shelters, as a last resort. Cut out a small hole for your face and pull it over your head. Tuck it in neatly around you and sit on it, using the rope or your rucksack to insulate you from the ground. Pull your rucksack up over your legs. If the bag is large enough for two people, the warmth factor increases considerably.

Shock

With anything more than a minor injury or accident, it is safe to assume that the patient will have suffered some degree of shock. As well as the actual casualty, other members of the party should be closely monitored in case they, too, develop the symptoms of shock.

The initial signs of shock are:

- A rapid pulse.
- Pale, grey skin. A fingernail or earlobe, if pressed, does not regain its colour immediately.
- Sweating and cold, clammy skin.

As the shock develops, patients will become weak, giddy and nauseous. They may vomit, and their breathing becomes rapid and shallow. The pulse continues to be fast but irregular. If the patient is not treated, they will become restless, anxious or aggressive. They may suffer 'air hunger', yawning and gasping for air. In the most severe cases they may become unconscious and eventually the heart will stop beating.

The treatment for shock is simple and effective. Treat the obvious cause of shock, such as bleeding or burns. Lie the casualty down, keeping the head low and raising the feet to aid the supply of blood to the brain. Loosen any tight clothing, belts or equipment. Keep the casualty warm and insulated, give plenty of reassurance and send for help.

Do not let the casualty move about, eat, drink or smoke. If they complain of being thirsty, moisten their lips with water.

Hypothermia

Hypothermia or exposure, as it is commonly known, is one of the great killers on the hills, but it can usually be avoided. It is caused by a combination of wet and cold, which can be aggravated by factors such as tiredness, inadequate clothing, inadequate diet and physical and mental attitude. Prevention is largely a matter of common sense.

Before going on the climb ensure that:

- All members of the group are correctly clothed and equipped.
- Everyone has had a decent breakfast, and has an adequate supply of food and drink (including emergency rations).
- The weather conditions are suitable for your planned trip.
- The planned trip is within the physical and mental capabilities for all members of the group.
- Nobody in the group is suffering from a severe cold or 'flu or any other condition which makes the planned trip unsuitable for them.

On the trip the members of the group should keep an eye on each other. No matter how bad the conditions get, it is vital to keep talking to each other. Hypothermia often goes unnoticed until too late.

The signs of hypothermia include:

- Shivering and cold, pale marble-like skin.
- Apathy, confusion and irrational or 'drunken' behaviour.
- Complaining of tiredness, coldness, cramp (particularly in the calf muscles) or blurred vision.

Many of these symptoms could also be attributed to being merely 'cold, wet and tired'. The key to early recognition of hypothermia depends upon knowing the members of your group and detecting behaviour that is out of character. The later signs, such as loss of faculties and blurred vision, are more obvious but the patient's health will already have deteriorated by the time these symptoms are displayed, and the aim is to arrest hypothermia at a much earlier stage.

The treatment for hypothermia:

- Stop at once. There is no point in pushing on unless you are very close to your base.
- Provide shelter from the elements. The priority is to get the casualty out of the wind or rain.
- Provide insulation from above and below.
- Start gentle rewarming. Placing another person in a sleeping bag with the casualty is a good method.
- Send for help.

You should never give the patient alcohol; nor should you attempt to rewarm the casualty rapidly by rubbing the skin or applying hot water bottles or any other form of direct heat. Give the patient a hot drink, soup or small amounts of high-energy food, such as chocolate, so long as there are not abdominal injuries. If there are other injuries, be cautious about food and drink but remember that hypothermia is often a bigger problem than the injury that started the situation. Wet clothes should only be removed in a warm sheltered environment and only if there are dry clothes immediately at hand.

Always assume that you and the other members of the group are also suffering from the initial stages of hypothermia and treat everyone accordingly. Remember: shelter, warmth and high morale are what you need to maintain while you wait for help.

Frostbite

Frostnip, and the more serious condition of frostbite, can be treated by gentle rewarming if spotted early enough. The first signs are pins and needles in the affected parts, which become pale and numb. Frostnip is quite common and is not a problem if treated. Frostbite, however, goes deeper into the body tissue, which turns hard, white and stiff, then mottled blue and eventually black.

In both cases it is vital to seek medical help as soon as possible. Make no attempt to thaw out the affected part until there is no risk of refreezing, but seek warm surroundings as rapidly as possible. Gently remove gloves, boots, socks, rings or watches and warm the affected parts with your hands, or in your lap or in the patient's own armpits. Warm water can be used, but take care when drying the affected parts – do not use pressure or burst any blisters.

Acute mountain sickness

Acute mountain sickness (AMS) is a very serious, but specialized, condition caused by the effects of high altitude. Proper training and information are vital if you intend climbing at high altitude.

Heat exhaustion

Heat exhaustion results from dehydration and salt loss because of excessive sweating. It can be caused by other conditions, such as diarrhoea or vomiting. Patients suffering from heat exhaustion will complain of dizziness, headaches, cramps and loss of appetite or nausea. The skin will be clammy, sweaty and pale. Move the patient to cool, shaded surroundings, preferably with a breeze. Help the patient to lie down, then raise and support the legs to promote blood flow to the brain. Give the patient as much salt solution (2 teaspoons of salt per 1 litre/2 pints of cool water) as they can drink. If recovery is slow, or if the patient's breathing and pulse remain rapid, seek immediate medical advice.

Sprained ankles

Along with blisters (see page 113), sprained ankles are one of the most common injuries. Although some sprains are major and very painful, most can be walked on after simple treatment and care. Prompt treatment is very much the key to treatment of any sprain injury.

Treatment is summed up in the mnemonic RICE:

Rest.
Ice (cooling the injured area in any suitable way).
Compression (strapping the ankle).
Elevation (raising the foot).

To strap an ankle: use an elastic or crêpe bandage, start inside the instep of the foot and wrap the bandage tightly (but not too tightly) over the foot and around the ankle, continuing in a figure-of-eight around the foot and ankle until the foot is well supported. If possible, replace the boot to give additional support. Paracetamol can help with pain relief.

Fractures

Fractures can be classified as those you can treat and walk with and those you cannot.

In the case of a minor fracture (for example of the arm, fingers or collar bone), there is usually no need to call out a rescue party. The fracture should be supported in whatever position the casualty finds most comfortable and restrained from further movement. Fingers can be strapped to each other, while a broken arm can be supported in a sling and then strapped to the body. A collar bone is treated in the same manner as if the arm on that side were broken. Minor foot, leg or ankle injuries can be treated similarly if the group is capable of helping the casualty back off the hill.

If the fracture cannot be treated you should make the patient as comfortable as possible and summon help. If it is necessary to immobilize a limb to prevent the condition becoming worse, the best option is to use other body parts – strapping the legs together, for example. To do this, you need to place cushioning material between the legs, especially at the knees and ankles, then bandage the legs together, tying the knots on the side of the uninjured leg. Check that the bandages are not too tight by pinching a toe nail: if it stays pale, loosen and retie the bandages.

Do not give food or drink to the patient, in case they need an emergency operation to reset the bones.

Dislocations

Dislocations can be very painful and require expert help. The exception, as with fractures, is in minor cases where the affected limb can be supported and the patient can still walk. Some people have a history of dislocations and sometimes know how to treat themselves by pushing the joint back in. This is very rare and is not something you should attempt.

Chronic conditions

You should always be aware if any member of your party suffers from a chronic condition such as asthma, diabetes or epilepsy. In each case it is vital that you know how to deal with any problems that might arise, and that you have adequate supplies of medicines and inhalers. Asthma sufferers should carry and use their own inhalers rather than a communal one.

Bites and stings

Bites and stings vary greatly from the intense annoyance caused by the Scottish midge to the lethal effects of some snakes and marine life.

Black flies, midges, no-see-'ems and sand flies all have an unpleasant bite which is best avoided by keeping well covered and staying inside your tent at dusk and dawn, when they are most active. Repellent creams are not very effective and can harm your skin. Antihistamine lotions and pills may help to reduce the itching from insect bites but should not be used to excess.

Stings from insects (such as wasps and bees) or sea creatures (such as jellyfish, weaver fish or anemones) are usually more painful than dangerous, but be alert to multiple stings which have dangerous cumulative effects, stings to the mouth or throat that can swell and block the airway, and stings to people who develop an allergic reaction.

For a sting to the mouth, give the patient ice to suck if at all possible to reduce the swelling and get them to hospital. Multiple stings and allergic reactions manifest themselves in the same way: red blotchy skin, facial swelling and puffiness around the eyes, impaired breathing and a rapid pulse. Get the patient to hospital as rapidly as possible. If the patient remains conscious, help them to find the most comfortable position for breathing freely. If unconscious, put the patient in the recovery position (see page 105).

Bites from venomous snakes are treated by laying the casualty down with the bite at the lowest possible level. Wash the wound as well as you are able and keep the patient as calm and still as possible while help is summoned. Identification of the snake is a help but do not put yourself at risk in order to do so. Never apply a tourniquet, cut the wound or try to suck out the poison.

Blisters

Blisters are there for a reason: the liquid they contain serves to protect and cool the wound. This is the body's way of coping with an injury such as a friction burn and no attempt should be made to drain a blister. Instead, cover the blister with gauze pads and tape or plasters. If the blister has burst by itself *do not* remove the broken skin, as this will only leave a delicate, unprotected area. Cover the area with plenty of padding. The key to both blister prevention and blister treatment is prompt action: there is no point in hoping that the pain will go away if you keep going.

Do not forget that blisters can be caused by badly fitting, inadequate or damp socks, so carry spare socks. Another item that is well worth carrying (if you can justify the weight) is a pair of thongs or flip-flops so that you can get out of your boots in the evening and let your feet relax. Look after your feet and they will look after you.

7

Training and fitness

Climbing can place great demands on both body and mind. Some investment in fitness training and the cultivation of a positive attitude will
make your climbing both more successful and more enjoyable.

Fitness

To climb well, you should be able to combine strength, endurance and
flexibility.

Strength

You need arm strength to haul your body-weight over a strenuous overhang. You need finger strength to hold on to small fingerholds on steep
rock. You not only need strength in your legs and back when walking
uphill to the cliff, you also need it to make high steps on a climb and to
hold the body in a strenuous bridging position across a groove or chimney. Strength allows you to apply a force in a desired direction and will
usually involve either moving or supporting your body-weight. Clearly,
what is important is not the absolute degree of strength that you can
deploy, but rather how much strength you can apply for your weight.
Some very slimly built people have a tremendous strength-to-weight ratio
whereas the obvious strength of, for instance, a rugby player would, in a
climbing situation, have to be used to haul his bulk against the drag of
gravity.

Endurance

Endurance is what allows you to keep using your strength for more than
a few seconds. The climber experiences it in different ways. There is a
general level of aerobic endurance that would, for instance, allow you to
run for a few kilometres or swim for half an hour. This same endurance
is what will get you up a long pitch.

Aerobic refers to the fact that muscles are supplied with oxygen
throughout the period that they are being used. If the supply of oxygen
is inadequate, either because you are working the muscles so hard or
because the supply of oxygenated blood is restricted by gravity or muscle
tension, then the muscles have to function *anaerobically*, that is, without

114

oxygen. When muscles function in this way they produce metabolic products such as lactic acid which accumulate and cause discomfort, lack of strength and cramping. The climber hanging on small fingerholds on steep rock will rapidly feel the onset of this unless in peak condition.

Watch climbers on steep rock and you will see them frequently take off a hand and 'shake out' below waist level before changing over and shaking out the other hand. This restores the blood flow to the muscles of the inner forearm that flex the fingers. When you are unfit and lack endurance your muscles will quickly knot up and will take a considerable time to recover, if they do so at all. When you are fit, your muscles work for a longer period before cramping and when the blood flow is restored they recover much more quickly. Some climbs make great demands on the feet and legs but the main focus of endurance training is likely to be on the fingers and arms.

Flexibility

Flexibility will allow you to position your body in the optimum way to make use of the holds and to apply your strength in the most efficient manner. If you lack flexibility in the hips, you will suffer agonies on climbs that involve sustained wide bridging and are likely to find high step-ups very difficult. Watch skilled and flexible climbers and note how they can step up onto holds that are at waist level or above before flowing their body effortlessly up onto this new support point.

A few weeks after I started climbing, I got hold of a book which described how to climb Slingsby's Chimney on Scafell. Part of the description has stayed with me:

Many leaders fail to find the crucial hidden handhold. This reduces their ascent to a grunting and ungainly struggle.

'Grunting' and 'ungainly' can hardly be bettered as adjectives for those who climb without flexibility. They may climb ferociously difficult climbs but they will have to use more strength and more endurance than the subtle and flexible operator.

Training

The best general training for climbing is climbing. If you are lucky enough to be able to climb three days a week and combine this with some bouldering and some running to develop your aerobic fitness, then you will find your fitness steadily improves.

If you intend to go further with training, you can develop both strength and endurance on a climbing wall, possibly combined with a regime of weight training. However, you should be aware that if you approach this kind of training in the wrong way you can easily sustain an injury that can put you out of action for a frustratingly long time.

Always start from a good general level of fitness based on running, swimming or similar activities, but also invest some time in stretching and warming up. Static exercises, designed to stretch relaxed muscles and undertaken before exercise, will greatly reduce your chance of injury and over a period of weeks will start to increase your flexibility.

Climbing walls

The provision of climbing walls is a growth area in the leisure industry and many major cities now have large and elaborate ones. At the other end of the scale, many climbers have equipped a garage wall with bolt-on holds or have screwed small holds made of hardwood onto substantial plywood panels. This latter form is very simple to construct and can easily be made to tilt to varying angles if it is supported by a suitable frame.

Purpose-made climbing walls (figure 7.1) vary tremendously in quality. The best offer a wide variety of different types of hold and different moves, ranging from slabs to overhanging walls and roofs, with a bouldering area and sections equipped with bolts where people can lead. If the wall is climbed by top roping or leading, then a number of climbable lines are likely to exist for a particular rope station. Sometimes these are colour-coded so that, for instance, the green holds are an easy route but the blue holds much more difficult, or a grade and arrow may be painted at the foot of the rock. Most walls now have top ropes *in situ*: you simply tie onto one end and your partner belays the other with their belay plate. From the top, you can then be lowered down, although it is sometimes good endurance training actually to climb down and then climb back up again. The system on leading walls is very like that used on sport climbs but will sometimes have quick-draws in place.

Climbing walls provide an all-weather gymnasium for climbers and they offer a remarkably enjoyable alternative to the crags themselves if it is pouring with rain outside .

You do not need much equipment to climb on a wall – your harness, belay plate, screwgate karabiner, chalk bag, and rock boots and light, flexible clothing together with a fleece jacket or sweatshirt to wear when you are resting. Check the rules of your local wall to find out whether you need to take your own rope and quick-draws for leading.

Most walls have the floor padded with crash mats. Under bouldering walls with desperate roofs, these mats are of very deep foam (rather like the pits that high jumpers land in) but the main parts of climbing walls tend to have much thinner mats. These certainly reduce the possibility of

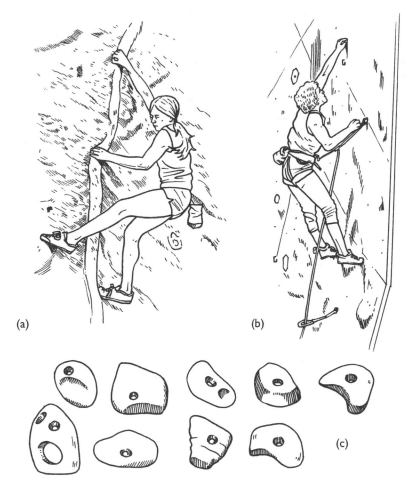

7.1 Climbing walls: (a) bouldering wall; (b) leading wall; (c) bolt on hold.

injury, but you can still break something if you land awkwardly or jump from a height.

When you arrive at the wall, fight off the temptation to hurl yourself at the steepest and most difficult climb there. Spend a bit of time stretching and then warm up by climbing rapidly on fairly easy climbs. Stretches which affect the Achilles tendon, the quadriceps, the hamstrings, hips, back, shoulders and neck are useful ones for the rock climber (figure 7.2). You should start out on climbs with large holds and not go on to tiny fingerholds until you and your large muscle groups are properly warmed up.

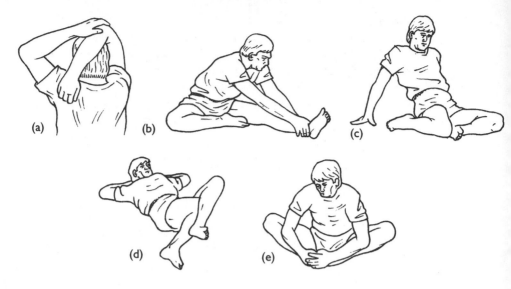

7.2 Some stretches: (a) shoulders; (b) hamstrings; (c) quadriceps; (d) hips; (e) groin.

Strength training

To train for strength, find a section of the wall that uses the right muscles and which you find quite, but not extremely, difficult. Now repeat the move a number of times with no resting until you can do it no more (but do avoid struggling – this is when you are likely to hurt yourself). Rest for a few minutes and then repeat the process; rest again and repeat once more. It is the last few repeats, when fatigue is very evident, which are the most effective training.

Endurance training

To develop endurance, particularly in the fingers and arms, you should aim to stay off the floor for as long as possible. Traversing vertical walls on small fingerholds until you can simply hang on no longer, resting and repeating and resting and repeating, will have dramatic effects on your endurance. However, be extremely careful not to overdo finger training (figure 7.3). It is very easy to damage joints and tendons through overuse. Some people tape their fingers with support tape to protect against tendon damage, but more moderate use is probably a better solution. Above all, avoid getting into a rut. Try to use a variety of holds – big ones and small ones; make strenuous moves and delicate ones; and do not forget to use your brain as well as your muscles. Climbing walls can be extremely useful at teaching you to solve climbing problems quickly.

Weight training

Weight training is a specialist activity and I would recommend you to take advice from a coach or one of the specialist books in this field. You should select a regime that helps you to develop strength and endurance rather than the kind of muscle bulk that body-builders might seek.

Two simple ways of improving your finger strength and endurance are to use finger exercisers or a 'roll-up'. *Finger exercisers* are either spring-loaded gadgets to be compressed between the fingers, or you can simply squeeze a squash ball. Hold the gadget above your head, because that is where your hand will be when you are climbing, and compress it repeatedly. Do not stop when it starts to hurt – just keep going until you can go on no longer. Then change hands. By the time your other arm is finished, the first will be ready for a repeat.

A *roll-up* (see figure 7.3) is a length of broomstick about 20cm (8in) in length attached by 1m (3ft) of nylon cord to a weight of about 3 kg (7lb). Hold the broomstick at arm's length in both hands and turn it to wind the weight up. When the weight is up, let it down gradually (dropping it is considered cheating) until it is just above the ground, and then repeat. If you do these exercises on a regular basis you will soon be cracking walnuts with your bare fingers!

7.3 Building those fingers – roll-ups.

Mental attitude

Mind and body are not separate in climbing; they are interconnected and interdependent. On any pitch, a climber is balancing risk against possibility and anxiety against determination and previous experience. If you are able to climb with a confident and positive approach, you exert less force with your muscles (you do not 'hang on for dear life') and you will not experience the demoralizing and enervating effects of too high a level of anxiety.

Interestingly, few of us climb at our best on easy climbs because a certain level of anxiety seems to be necessary to give the mind a sharp focus and to trigger some of the body's helpful physiological mechanisms. Raise the anxiety to a state of real fear and the results are dramatic. You feel strength draining from your arms, your balance deteriorates and you tend to lean in and clutch the rock. Your attention span diminishes and your pulse races. The signals you are getting are completely clear and if you allow your anxieties to take over it is likely to result in a fall.

You will inevitably find yourself in situations where climbing a section is more difficult than anticipated, or a hold breaks or whatever, but with experience and a robust mental approach you can absorb these difficulties without upsetting your background mental state. Paradoxically, on many hard climbs and especially on solo climbs, it is the very fear of falling that is most likely to result in a fall taking place.

Concentrating on the positive will not make the setbacks disappear, but it may put them in proper perspective. Very often, a positive approach to difficulties is to identify what you can do in order to overcome them, and this might involve training or one of the other strategies mentioned in the table opposite.

Many of these ideas are simply mental games and you may or may not find them useful. The really important step is to recognize that you can affect your own mental attitude and that this in turn has a huge effect on the success and enjoyment of your climbing. To lead a long, difficult pitch in magnificent surroundings with control and deep concentration is one of life's peak experiences.

Health and nutrition

The best climbers will approach issues of health and diet with the same seriousness as any top-line athlete. For the recreational climber, probably the most important aspect is to avoid destroying your hard-won strength-to-weight ratio by putting on the kilos. Most of the best modern climbers are *ectomorphs*. This sounds as though they are pieces of protoplasm from outer space (maybe that is their secret), but in fact this is a physiological term referring to a tall, slim, long-boned build. With

Various strategies can be used to develop an effective mental attitude:

- Develop a regular routine at the start of a pitch. For instance, you can check your knots and harness and organize your gear in the same way just before starting any pitch. This meditative interlude will calm you up to the point where you give yourself the green light and start climbing.
- Ensure that the first few metres of a pitch go smoothly. Make sure that your boots are clean, that you know exactly where the route goes and that you have spotted where the first resting place or runner is situated.
- Deal with a long climb one pitch at a time and break down each pitch into convenient chunks between runners or resting places.
- When you have placed and clipped a secure runner, identify your next goal (the runner or resting place) and concentrate your attention on climbing smoothly and effectively to that point.
- As anxiety builds and you feel your muscles tensing, try to relax by taking a few deep breaths before moving on. Do not hold your breath whilst climbing.
- Identify what makes you anxious and work to diminish its effect. If you are scared of your fingers opening up, then concerted finger training will diminish your anxiety.
- At the start of a difficult pitch, visualize your progress up it in the way that you would wish to climb. Think upward!
- Imagine yourself 'flowing' across the rock, just touching holds like a spider or a dancer.
- Make your own mental dialogue take place in positive terms. Say to yourself, 'Relax, climb well,' rather than, 'Don't fall off.'
- Emphasize to yourself the positive achievements of your climbs not the setbacks. Thus: 'I climbed over 300m (980ft) at 5a standard today in a relaxed and successful way,' rather than, 'I made a complete mess of those 2m (6ft) of 5b, I'm never going to be a decent climber.'

proper training, such a build will have an excellent strength-to-weight ratio. If you naturally incline towards stockiness or worse, you will need to take care that nature's weight belt does not hold you back too much.

A balanced, high protein diet with plenty of fresh fruit and vegetables but low in saturated fats will help you to be both slim and healthy. Climbing is a very physical activity and if you try to lose excessive amounts of weight you will undoubtedly adversely affect your strength and endurance. Without proper vitamins, you will find that jamming scars and minor abrasions tend to heal poorly. In any case, you will find that it is difficult to climb well after a large meal so concentrate your eating in the evenings with a light lunch and breakfast. In hot climates, make sure that your fluid intake is adequate for the conditions.

It is obvious that alcohol and other drugs diminish your reaction time and affect your judgement, but you should also be aware that medications can have a similar effect. In particular, I have found that a number of climbers who use antihistamine medication for allergic conditions find that their concentration is very seriously affected. The safest plan is to avoid using the medicine or, if this is not possible, only to climb second on the rope.

Women and climbing

To include a section with such a title is something of an anachronism nowadays but, as in other previously male-dominated activities, sexist attitudes still exist. Unfortunately, some unreconstructed males continue to regard women as decorative seconds with no leading ambitions of their own. If you find that a male climbing partner cramps your style or if he sees your success as a threat to his delicate ego, then you should find a different partner.

Climbing walls must have helped to increase the proportion of female climbers by letting women see that flexibility and balance rather than sheer brute force are often the key to success on even the hardest climbs. Women such as Catherine Destivelle and the late Alison Hargreaves have completed climbs in the Alps that put them amongst the first rank of climbers of either gender and the gap between top-level male and female performers in climbing-wall competitions is much narrower than in many sports.

8

Advanced techniques

To be safe and efficient as a climber you need to have a complete command of the basic techniques and systems. This chapter deals with a variety of topics that might be useful when you have been climbing for a while, but are certainly not essential in the early stages.

Falls and forces

Seventy kilograms (155lb) of climber accelerating downwards at 9.81m per second squared develops an impressive amount of energy that the belay system has to absorb. The most useful theory covering this is based on the assumption that most of the energy of a fall is absorbed in the elasticity of the rope. Modern climbing ropes display considerable elasticity and can stretch by 60 per cent of their length before breaking.

Fall factors

The fall factor (figure 8.1) is defined as:

$$\frac{\text{length of fall}}{\text{length of rope absorbing the fall}}$$

Example 1

A leader who has placed no protection, falling when 5m (16ft) above the second, will fall for a total of 10m (33ft) to a point 5m (16ft) below the belayer. Therefore:

$$\text{Fall factor} = \frac{\text{length of fall}}{\text{length of rope out}} = \frac{10\text{m (33ft)}}{5\text{m (16ft)}} = FF\,2$$

The interesting thing about the physics of this theory is that the force developed in the system (the impact force) depends only on the fall factor. This means that a total fall of 40m (130ft) from 20m (65ft) above the belay, again without any runners in place, will still be of fall factor 2 and the force on the belayer and the anchors will be identical to that in the first example. Unfortunately, this does not mean that the risk to the leader does not increase. The longer the fall, the greater the velocity developed and the greater the chance of hitting a ledge or an obstruction.

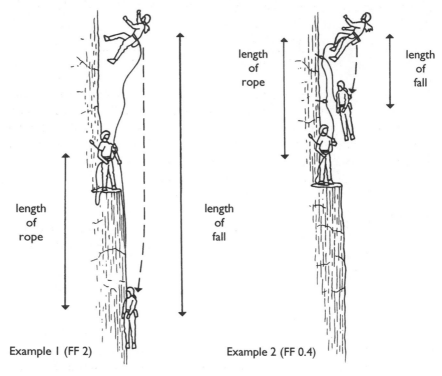

Example 1 (FF 2)   Example 2 (FF 0.4)

8.1 Fall factors.

Example 2

Imagine, in Example 1, that the leader has placed a runner 4m (13ft) up the pitch and falls off when 1m (3ft) higher. In this case:

$$\text{Fall factor} = \frac{\text{length of fall}}{\text{length of rope out}} = \frac{\text{2m (6ft)}}{\text{5m (16ft)}} = \text{FF} \, 0.4$$

A factor 2 fall places a severe strain on the falling climber, the belayer and the safety chain. In the case where the runner is placed, because the impact force is proportional to the fall factor, a fall factor of 0.4 will generate in the system a maximum force only 20 per cent of that from the fall without a runner (fall factor 2). This is why it is absolutely essential to place a secure runner early on a pitch.

Example 3

Return to Example 1, with the leader 5m (16ft) above the second without runners. This time, when the leader falls the second is extremely efficient and manages to take in 2.5m (8ft) of rope while the fall is taking place.

$$\text{Fall factor} = \frac{\text{length of fall}}{\text{length of rope out}} = \frac{7.5\text{m (25ft)}}{2.5\text{m (8ft)}} = \text{FF}\,3$$

The well-intentioned action of the second in taking in rope has actually increased the already severe forces in the system by a further 50 per cent. **You should not attempt to take in the rope during a fall without runners unless there is a clear risk of the falling climber hitting an obstacle below.** In that case, the increased forces in the system are preferable to the danger of a high-speed impact.

Example 4

As a final example, consider a leader falling off 5m (16ft) above a secure runner near the top of a long pitch with 40m (130ft) of rope extended:

$$\text{Fall factor} = \frac{\text{length of fall}}{\text{length of rope out}} = \frac{10\text{m (33ft)}}{40\text{m (130ft)}} = \text{FF}\,0.25$$

Ten metres (33ft) is quite a long fall, but because so much rope is extended, the force developed in the system is relatively small. This tells us that **as long as there is no danger of hitting an obstruction it is safe to widen the spacing between successive runners as you progress up a pitch. Correspondingly, it is wisest to concentrate runners in the first third of a pitch.**

These calculations are all theoretical and they ignore, for instance, slippage by the belayer or the friction developed in the karabiners or runners. However, most of these factors work to reduce the maximum force in the system so fall factors represent a useful 'worst case' analysis and give very good guidance about optimal protection of a pitch.

The actual force developed in the system also depends on the elasticity of the rope. This does not vary greatly but the UIAA test statistics for a rope quote a quantity called *impact force*. A quoted impact force of 1070 kiloponds represents a much less stretchy rope than one of 9050 kiloponds, so the first rope will develop greater forces in the system for the same length of fall.

Acclimatization

On steep, well-protected climbs the risks to a falling leader are generally well controlled. The fear of falling is one of the strongest factors limiting maximum performance. Therefore climbers at the highest standard deliberately acclimatize themselves and become relaxed about the possibility of falling off. This is fine, but be aware that you are placing enormous trust in the protection system that you have set up and must be absolutely sure that no component part of it is likely to fail.

Belaying

The system of belaying described in Chapter 4 is called an *indirect belay* because, in the event of a fall, the body of the belaying climber is interposed in the system between the rope loaded by the fallen climber and the main anchors. If the belayer is correctly positioned this provides very helpful shock absorption and can protect a less-than-perfect anchor.

In some circumstances a *direct belay* can be used. Here, the force from the falling climber is absorbed directly by an anchor. At its simplest, in alpine or scrambling situations, the rope is simply passed around a spike or block. In experienced hands the friction of the rope on rock is sufficient to hold a second's fall, but this cannot be recommended as a reliable method.

I never use direct belays for belaying a leader, but in the right circumstances it is a very convenient way of top roping a single-pitch climb. The essential is an absolutely bombproof anchor, such as a large tree equipped with a full-weight sling and screwgate karabiner. If the anchor point is roughly at shoulder level, my method of choice is to use the Munter hitch as this provides the ideal amount of friction. If the climber falls, they can be easily lowered to the start of the pitch under the control of the belayer using the Munter hitch. Belay plates are not convenient to use for direct belays unless they are at a low level relative to the belayer. This will allow the control rope to be at the optimum angle of 120–180 degrees to the loaded rope.

Direct belays are occasionally useful, but there are no arguments for substituting them for indirect belays in the majority of climbing situations.

Double ropes

Your two half ropes should be of different colours (red and blue, for example) and be uncoiled into separate heaps. Half ropes are usually 8.5mm or 9mm (⅓ or ⅜in) in diameter, but it is perfectly feasible to climb on a 9mm (⅜in) plus an 11mm (⅜in), although this is heavier and you will require a belay plate that is compatible with this arrangement.

Straightforward pitches

If the pitch that you are climbing follows a fairly straight course, as might be the case on a crack climb, then you would normally alternate the ropes through runners. The advantage of this is that, should you fall, it would be quite common for both the top runners to take your weight with consequently less strain on each one. It is possible to use quite a lot of energy in pulling up rope to clip into a runner and, if you slip at this point, the rope you have pulled up will increase the length of your fall. By using double ropes the protection from your last runner is unaffected by pulling rope through to clip into the new runner. Ideally, however, you should avoid clipping in until the runner is at waist level.

Problems
Irregular distribution of runners
If you are climbing a pitch in which the distribution of runners is more irregular, then roughly separate them into 'left-hand' runners and 'right-hand' runners and clip the red rope into one set and the blue rope into the other. Very often, simply separating the runners in this way will greatly reduce the possibility of rope drag and you may not need to extend any runners (except for wires where the use of short extensions is standard practice). If a runner is out of line with those that precede and those that are likely to follow it, then extend it with a longer sling.

Twisted ropes
As you clip each runner, check that the rope below is running cleanly and freely and that you have not accidentally put a twist in the ropes. If twists do get into the system it is usually inconvenient rather than disastrous, but it does increase friction and can tend to lift out runners.

Traversing
When a pitch has some distinct sections of traversing in it (figure 8.2), then you may clip the red rope into five or six runners in one crack system, saving the blue rope until you have traversed into a second crack. The considerate leader should also be looking for opportunities to protect the second person on the rope: double ropes can greatly assist this where traverses or short descents occur.

Poor protection
On a poorly protected pitch, you will often find a placement for a runner which is quite obviously going to be the last for a considerable distance. If the placement permits, then place at least two runners, each clipped to a different rope. This means that, should you have a longish fall from the unprotected section, the impact will be absorbed by two ropes and two runners and improve your chances accordingly. Take care that there is no risk of the krabs of the adjacent runners opening each other.

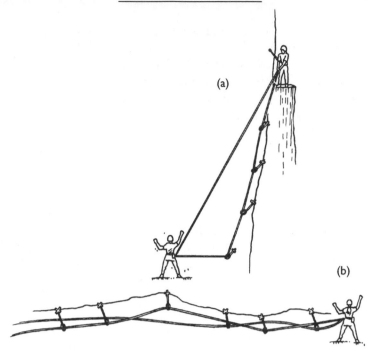

8.2 Double ropes on a traverse. (a) The second is protected from above and (b) the leader alternately clips each rope.

For the second climber, the use of double ropes is a little more difficult and you must learn to be adept at feeding out and taking in the ropes independently. It is of great assistance to the leader if, when you sense that a runner is being clipped, you feed out the correct rope freely. You should also slightly modify the calls; for example you might shout, 'That's me on blue, take in red', and so on.

Very occasionally, on long and complex pitches, a rope will sometimes jam solidly. When climbing on a double rope you can, as a last resort, untie from one rope and complete the pitch on the remaining free rope. Finally, double ropes have clear benefits in areas of loose rock or sharp flakes, since if one rope is damaged there is a good chance that the other will remain intact.

Sport climbing

Sport-climbing areas are ones where most of the climbs are of a single pitch and are predominantly bolt-protected. Such areas give climbing of tremendous technical interest and an atmosphere and ethos midway between climbing walls and traditional crags. Usually, the bolts mark the line of the route very clearly and where the pitch ends there will be an anchor from which the climber can be lowered off. This is often two bolts linked by a chain or, better still, what is called a *cold clip*.

Sport climbers (figure 8.3) usually climb on a single full rope which is often uncoiled onto a rope bag or sheet of nylon to protect it from grit. Because you are climbing on single ropes you are placing a great deal of trust in a single bolt and in the person that placed it. Your rack is usually no more than a bundle of quick-draws sufficient to clip all the bolts on the pitch.

Efficiency in clipping protection bolts can make a big difference on a strenuous climb and so sport climbers tend to use karabiners of a special-ized design with particularly easy handling and clipping characteristics. It is helpful if the karabiner which is to take the rope is firmly located in the quick-draw and this can be achieved by using a rubber band, tight stitching or even by having a captive eye forged in the karabiner. At the other end, it is useful if the karabiner that clips the bolt can be turned around and arranged so that the gate is away from the rock. The 'bolt' krab is often chosen in the form of a straight gate to reduce accidental unclipping, whereas the 'rope' krab is bent-gate to ease clipping of the rope. The bolt krab often becomes burred. This will damage the rope if used as a rope krab.

Occasionally, you see people using either a single karabiner in a bolt or two karabiners clipped together, but both of these arrangements have some risk of the karabiner twisting and opening accidentally.

Pitches are rarely more than 25m (80ft) in height so the leader can be lowered back down to the ground before the second starts to climb. To do this, the leader clips his rope into the cold clip (the most satisfactory arrangement since it does not require the leader to untie) and is lowered off by the second. In some areas a fixed ring is in place and the leader has to untie and thread the rope through this before retying onto the rope. This is a moment fraught with hazard and it is sensible to have an independent *cow's tail* – a length of tape attached directly to your harness and culminating in a screwgate karabiner. You should double-check that you are secured by your cow's tail before untying the rope and make sure that you do not drop the rope.

Once clipped in by your cow's tail, an elegant solution is to pull up some slack rope and thread a bight through the lower-off point. Tie a fig-ure-of-eight loop in this bight and attach it with a screwgate to your har-ness. now untie your main tie-on knot and pull the loose end through the lower-off. You can now unclip the cow's tail and be lowered off. This is more complicated but eliminates the risk of dropping the rope. Most commonly, the leader is lowered to the ground and then the second

8.3 Sport climbing: preparing to clip the rope into an extender clipped to a bolt on a fierce roof. The second should give some slack at this stage but this does risk a longer fall.

follows the pitch and retrieves the equipment before being lowered in turn from the top anchor. Sometimes, if the second does not intend to follow the pitch, the leader can remove the quick-draws whilst being lowered down.

Sport climbing gives you a superb opportunity not only to develop your fitness and skill but also to cultivate a positive attitude.

Techniques

You will build up your own repertoire of techniques as you do more and more climbing, but here are a few that have not been mentioned so far.

Pinch grips

If you transfer to the rockface the kind of grip you would take on a book to remove it from a bookshelf, you are using a pinch grip (figure 8.4). The wider the angle of the piece of rock being pinched, the harder it becomes. To work effectively on, say, a right-angled arête requires both enormous strength and rock that gives good friction. It helps greatly if you can apply the pinch at a point where there is a local narrowing.

Sometimes it is easier to use an edge as a lay away (or layback) rather than a pinch grip.

Small fingerholds

It is best if you get the maximum number of fingers on a small hold even if this means 'stacking' the fingers by putting one above the other. Try to minimize the leverage on very small holds by applying the tips rather than the pads of the fingers to the hold and sharply hooking your fingers. Stacking fingers in a fingerjam is often called a *fingerlock*.

Footwork

Any support that your feet can give eases the strain on your arms and fingers. Even if you have run out of footholds, a high-friction boot *smeared* (figure 8.4) onto the rock can make a suprising difference. The more that you can lean out on your fingers, the more your feet are likely to adhere successfully.

Locking off

This very valuable skill is used on steep rock: you hold the upper body static with one bent arm whilst the other arm is either moved up to a higher hold or used to place protection (figure 8.4). Being able to 'lock off' in a kind of frozen pull-up is a great deal more valuable than being able to do large numbers of pull-ups themselves. However, do not overdo static hangs in training – they are particularly damaging to joints and tendons. Incidentally, if you have to hang from a hold to rest or place protection, it is much less strenuous to do so on a straight arm, where the strain is taken by the skeleton, than to do it on a bent arm, where the strain is taken by the muscles.

Down-climbing

Alpine climbers tend to get a lot of practice in down-climbing but it is often neglected by crag climbers. This is a pity because being able to down-climb a few moves after an unsuccessful attempt at a section of a climb is extremely useful. There are no secrets, but practice will pay dividends.

Dynos

The traditional, rather static view of climbing is that the climber should maintain three-point contact. Dynos, as their name suggests, are much more dynamic manoeuvres where the climber may part company from the rock altogether in a ballistic leap for a hold. It is worth practising this on a climbing wall before trying it on a big route and also worth check-

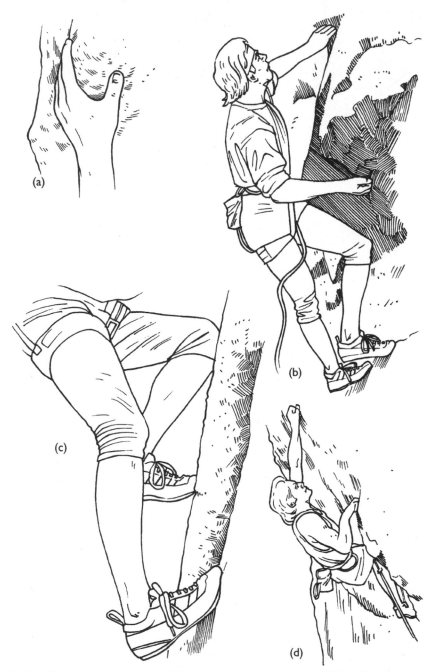

8.4 (a) Pinch grip on an arête. (b) Using an undergrip on an overhang. (c) 'Smearing' on poor footholds. (d) Locking off: the climber has locked off on the right arm and is reaching up for a hold with the left.

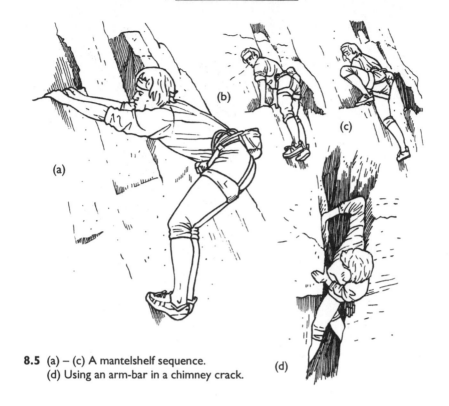

8.5 (a) – (c) A mantelshelf sequence.
(d) Using an arm-bar in a chimney crack.

ing that your target hold is a good one! The spring upwards should start from the feet.

In a more modest form, a similar technique is much more widely applicable. If you find yourself hanging on small fingerholds with difficulty in removing one hand in order to reach up to the next holds, let your body weight sink down and then extend upwards. You will be able to take one hand off while your body mass is still moving upwards.

Mantelshelves

I have never met anyone who confesses to liking mantelshelves. On traditional climbs, the manoeuvre consists of the climber pulling up on a narrow ledge, getting one foot onto it and then standing up with little assistance from the wall above (figure 8.5). On hard climbs mantelshelf moves are often on extremely sloping holds and may, for instance, be the culminating part of surmounting an overhang. You will find them easier if you have strong arms, shoulders and stomach muscles, but perhaps the greatest asset is an ability to grit your teeth and go for it!

Sprags

This minor technique (see figure 3.9 on page 39) can be useful in corners or certain cracks. Find a corner crack, about 3cm (1in) width, apply all your fingers, thumb down, along the edge of the crack and push hard with your thumb against the opposite wall. Often a sprag will give slightly more security than the layback or layaway that would work in the same place.

Overhangs

Overhangs are almost always strenuous and intimidating and once you are past a certain point on them it is very difficult to change your mind and come back. There is no standard technique but a few general principles may be useful.

General principles with overhangs:

---

1. Take advantage of any resting place before the overhang and at least 'shake out' your arms.
2. Place some good protection, remembering to extend this as necessary to avoid rope drag on the lip of the overhang.
3. Rest again and then move quickly upwards to minimize the time that you are hanging on your arms.
4. Often you will find undergrips beneath the overhang or on its lip (figure 8.4) and by using these it is possible to work your feet up high under the roof.
5. Then reach up for what you hope is going to be a good hold, first for one hand and then both.
6. Try to avoid your feet swinging off and keep them in contact with the rock as long as possible. As soon as you have handholds over the overhang, get your feet high and close to your hands before making what is, hopefully, the last move to a more comfortable position.

Some modern climbs cross the most astonishing ceilings with the climber hanging underneath horizontal rock for perhaps 5–10m (16–33ft).

Falling

If you fall off or are sure that you are about to, do not just give up. Concentrate very hard on getting a favourable outcome. If you are falling a relatively short way on to good protection, it is worth pushing out from the rock and then, as you swing back in underneath your runners, absorbing the impact with flexed arms and legs. As you part company with the rock it is worth shouting to wake up your second and trying to give yourself a trajectory that will miss any obvious obstructions. How you get on in a long fall is something of a lottery, but if you are climbing without a helmet, bunching up and protecting your head with your arms is probably worthwhile. I am assured that on extreme friction slabs, to avoid a buttock-searing slide down the slab, falling climbers have preferred to turn and sprint 30m (100ft) or more until the rope comes tight!

Poor rock

Crags are changing just as surely as the rest of the natural world, but their slow rate of change makes it easy for us to forget this. There are very few climbs of any length that do not have some loose rock on them and on some crags or rock types loose rock is the norm.

If a hold is loose your instincts will usually warn you and you can check by tapping or kicking the hold and listening to the sound generated. As long as you know that a hold is loose, it is often possible to use it safely if you make sure that you only load it in a direction that tends to keep it in position. Sometimes, when exploring new rock, you come across sections that are quite astonishingly loose and on occasions I have climbed on rock with such heavy horizontal fractures as to make the experience like climbing on precariously stacked library books.

Loose rock tends to be removed or stabilized with the passage of subsequent parties; for example, many of the climbs that were considered horrifically loose at the time of exploration of Craig Gogarth on Anglesey have now settled down to become frequently climbed classics with only occasional loose holds. If you find a loose hold with no useful adhesion to the crag it is probably best to remove this and throw it safely off the crag. In doing this, you must take care that there is no one underneath and, in any case, give a warning shout of 'Below!' or 'Rock!'

When climbing on loose or fragile rock it is prudent to spread your weight between several points of contact. The exhilarating one-arm swing that you might enjoy on solid rock might end rather suddenly. Finding secure protection is tricky. If the looseness is only at the level of individual holds, you will still often find secure and solid cracks in which to arrange good protection. If the looseness is on a larger scale, you may find that the only protection to be obtained is on the very flakes and blocks on which you are climbing and which are themselves insecure. On one climb in Norway I remember coming across a massive flake of rock, perhaps 10m (33ft) square, that appeared to have a crack running all the way round it. The only way to continue on the route was to chimney by back-and-footing between this flake and the main crag and the only protection on offer was on the flake itelf. It is very difficult to back-and-foot without placing any pressure on the side walls of a chimney!

If the only protection that you can find is on loose rock then you must climb with appropriate caution. You might improve the chances of a runner holding by, for instance, using a long extension so that the pull would be parallel with the rockface rather than outwards, or by using a large camming device which would, to some extent, expand with an expanding flake.

Sometimes rock is not loose at all but may be so brittle that small, sharp-edged holds or small pockets holding runners can break without warning.

Prusiks

The prusik knot is a way to tie a rope sling so that it will grip another rope (figure 8.6). The term has become a generic one to describe the wide variety of knots that can be used in this way. I believe that you can get by if you learn just one of these knots: the klemheist knot (figure 8.6).

Klemheist knot

The virtues of this knot are that it is simple to tie, will work with both rope or tape slings and rarely jams. The knot works best if tied using a 5 or 6mm ($\frac{1}{5}$ or $\frac{1}{4}$in) kernmantel sling on a single or double climbing rope. The difference in thickness between the sling and rope being gripped improves the friction being generated.

Take the end of the sling furthest from the knot and wind it in a downwards spiral around the climbing rope. After about four turns pass the long end of the sling through the loop at its starting end. Pull on the long end and you will find that the knot grips securely on the rope. The knot can be readily loosened and pushed up the rope as required. In some conditions three turns will give you sufficient grip. If the rope is muddy or icy you may need five turns. Some climbers are adept at tying this knot one-handed by flicking the knot of the sling around the rope.

Tie the knot with a tape sling in exactly the same way, but it will work best if you wind it so that the flat surface of the tape is in maximum contact with the rope.

Techniques with prusik knots

The main use of prusik knots is to allow the climber to ascend a rope in a self-rescue situation. Before doing this it is sensible to practise the basic technique.

The basic technique:

---

1. Tie both prusik loops on your rope with klemheist knots.
2. Attach the upper loop to the strong point at the front of your harness with a screwgate karabiner. The length of the link should be about 10cm (4in) and you will probably need to shorten the prusik loop by tying a figure-of-eight knot in it. You will use the lower loop as a footloop, either by standing directly in it or by putting a lark's foot around your boot.
3. Pull the climbing rope tight and slide your loops up as high as possible.
4. Sit in your harness, suspended from the upper loop, and strenuously stand up in the footloop. You can now slide the upper loop attached to your harness some distance up the taut rope.
5. Relax and sit back into your harness and then slide up the footloop. Keep repeating the process and you will gradually gain height.

Find a rock outcrop 6–8m (20–26ft) in height and hang a full-weight climbing rope down the crag from a secure anchor at its top. I use 5mm (⅕in) prusik loops of about 1mm (less than ¹⁄₁₀in) in circumference tied

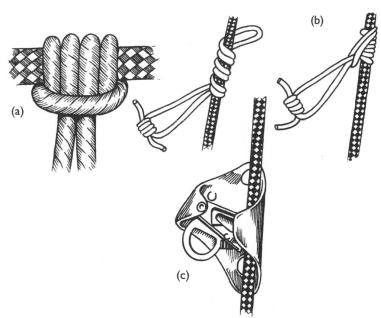

8.6 (a) Prusik knot. (b) Klemheist knot. (c) Mechanical ascender.

with a double fisherman's knot. Some people have the lower loop attached to the harness and the upper as the footloop, but I find that the method described is superior since the most awkward bit (moving up the loop attached to your sit-harness) is more easily done on the taut rope loaded by your footloop. Moving the footloop up the slack rope beneath you is no problem because you are sitting comfortably in your harness.

You are vulnerable when prusiking because the knots might slip or even break and so you should always be tied into the main rope in some way. On a long ascent every 5m (16ft) or so pull up the slack rope from below you, tie a figure-of-eight knot in it and clip it into a spare screw-gate karabiner on your harness. This way, if the prusiks fail, you will fall a relatively short distance to this back-up knot.

People who do a great deal of prusiking, such as cavers using single-rope techniques, or climbers of big walls, have developed more sophisticated ways of ascending a rope, but the method described is easy to use and easy to remember. I recommend it.

Mechanical ascenders

There are many purpose-made mechanical ascenders (figure 8.6) which use a camming system to grip the rope. They can be used in pairs and attached to you in exactly the same way as prusik loops. Be sure that you understand the safe use of the model of ascender that you are using.

Prusiks for self-belaying

There have been some nasty accidents where climbers have used a prusik loop attaching their harness to a fixed rope as a means of protecting themselves on solo climbs. If a fall occurs the prusik knot is quite incapable of absorbing the amount of energy generated. The loop can fuse all too easily and the climber then falls totally out of control. Even most purpose-made ascending devices are unsuitable for this use, so double-check to make absolutely certain that your manufacturer recommends its use as a protection device.

Self-rescue

A skilled climber can achieve remarkable feats of rope engineering with minimal equipment and most rock-climbing instructors are tested rigorously on these skills. However, to be done safely self-rescue requires a very good understanding and regular practice, so I would recommend that amateur climbers keep their repertoire of techniques to a minimum. If you want to know more, refer to one of the excellent specialist manuals on self-rescue. If someone in your party is seriously injured then you will need mountain rescue help (Chapter 6). If, however, members of your party are more or less able-bodied, you should be able to deal with most problem situations without calling on external help. Here are some of the scenarios.

Escape from a single pitch climb

You should be able to lower someone to the ground using your belay plate and then quickly descend the easy way to join them. Gear can be retrieved by abseil.

Retreat from a multi-pitch climb

Descend by abseil leaving secure anchors at convenient intervals. If you have been climbing on double ropes it is usually best to use the stances that you have used during your ascent. A single rope will not be long enough to permit this and intermediate anchors will be needed.

Sea cliff climb

The sea may prevent descent by abseil. If in difficulty your best hope is to force an ascent as described in the Weather section of Chapter 6, or seek help from a nearby party.

Fallen leader

If the leader is exhausted but uninjured and hanging from a runner, lower him to your belay ledge. He (or you!) may succeed on the pitch after a rest; otherwise, leave one or two high runners for security and have the leader strip the remainder whilst being lowered down. They will come in useful during your escape. Then proceed by abseiling or finding an easier route.

Caught by darkness

You cannot do very much in the dark unless you have head torches, so anticipate the problem sufficiently soon to do something about it, either by descending or by forcing a rapid ascent. If you can get one member of the party belayed at the top of the cliff before it is completely dark, then the rest of the party will usually manage to complete the ascent. If you are very near the top of a cliff as darkness encroaches, a top rope from another party can make a tremendous difference, but everyone needs to take particular care to ensure that their own safety is not compromised and that safe anchors and knots are used.

If all else fails, use the last of the light to establish your party on the most comfortable ledge you can find. Keep on harness and helmet and attach yourself securely to anchors. Wear all the clothing you have and sit on the spare rope for insulation. Huddle together for warmth. You will not pass a comfortable night but in most rock-climbing areas you should not be in undue danger during a relatively short summer night.

Climber hanging free

This is one of the difficult ones: either the leader or second has fallen off in an area of overhanging rock where they are completely out of contact with the rock. On a single-pitch climb they can be lowered to the ground, and on some multi-pitch climbs they may be lowered to an area of easier-angled rock where they can regain contact. Occasionally the belayer can throw a length of slack rope to pull in the hanging climber, but as a last resort prusiking techniques will have to be used.

Ideally you will be carrying a couple of prusik loops unobtrusively on your harness and these can now be brought into play and tied onto the rope close to your attachment point. If you do not have prusiks, you can use tape slings or anything else that is available. The film Les Abîmes has a chilling reconstruction of a huge fall on the Cima Ovest in the Italian Dolomites where the climber managed to use his bootlaces to prusik the full rope length in a position of appalling exposure. A fallen second can, if necessary, continue to prusik until reaching the stance, but the leader may only regain the runner which held the fall. From here the leader can consider the position and either go for a successful ascent or, with the second's help, return to the stance.

Protecting an abseil

One of the hazards not covered in Chapter 5 is the possibility of a climber losing control during an abseil. This could happen if you are taken ill, are hit by stonefall or are simply not concentrating. Since a safety rope is usually impractical in 'real' abseils, such eventualities can be very serious.

It is possible to guard against them by using a prusik knot. A klemheist knot is tied around the double abseil rope and attached with a link of about 40cm (15in) to your harness. The klemheist is cupped loosely in your non-control hand and the abseil proceeds normally (figure 8.7). If you are knocked out, you will let go of the klemheist knot and the control rope and the klemheist will lock and stop your fall. In principle, this should also guard against abseiling off the end of the rope, although this would be cutting things rather fine.

If the klemheist tightens accidentally, it can be very difficult to take your weight off it in order to recommence the abseil. For this reason, some climbers prefer to apply the klemheist to the control rope of the abseil and then tie the prusik onto, say, the rear of their harness. The advantage of this system is that the only tension on the klemheist is that

8.7 Protecting an abseil. (a) The climber clips the prusik loosely in the non-control hand, whilst descending. (b) This arrangement tightens on the control rope and so is easier to release under load.

necessary to lock the friction device and this is easily released. This would be another good way of taking both hands off to extract a jammed runner from an abseil.

In the event of your abseil rope jamming during retrieval, probably the best protection you can arrange is to use what slack rope you have to protect yourself as you climb up to the point where you can reach the doubled rope. At that point, apply your prusik loops around both ropes and ascend it by using the standard method until the blockage can be released.

Approach difficulties

Many sea cliffs and some climbs in river gorges can only be approached by abseil. You need to be doubly sure that you are starting your abseil from the correct point and take care to establish a secure anchor. In a popular climbing area you will often find a fixed anchor, usually festooned with large quantities of rotting slings. Since slings degrade in sunlight, it is sensible to replace anything that may have been there for more than a day or two.

If you have any doubts about your ability to make a successful ascent of the crag, you should take along a spare rope or ropes to leave on the abseil. Then, if your ascent is unsuccessful you at least have the option of ascending the abseil rope by prusiking. It would be normal to abseil on a single rope in this situation since you do not require to retrieve it from below.

When abseiling down, do so cautiously and check that the ends of your ropes reach a secure arrival point. If the descent is more than a single rope length, you must either find intermediate anchors (which prevent you from pulling the rope up from the top of the crag) or you must tie a second abseil rope onto the end of the first. Abseiling past a knot is very difficult if you are hanging free and you must take great care to ensure that you are securely attached to a prusik or ascender whilst moving your friction device past the knot.

Many of the techniques described above are ones that you may never use, but equally they can make the crucial difference in helping you to solve a particularly difficult problem.

9

Wider horizons

Exploration

One of the most exciting things in climbing is prospecting and completing a new route; in other words, climbing a line on the rock that no one has ever followed before. In popular climbing areas it is difficult to find unclimbed lines except at the highest standards, but people do regularly discover unclimbed middle-grade lines in the most unlikely places. The simplest time to discover new routes is just after a new edition of the guide book has been published, because then all the existing routes are clearly delineated. You may very well spot some unclimbed possibilities if you go along to an extensive crag and spend a few minutes comparing the lines on the crag with the recorded routes in the book.

It is very much easier to get to this stage in relatively unexplored areas and you may well find half a dozen potential new lines on any crag. Many climbers who operate regularly in such areas will have a mental file of these lines.

The really exciting part is when you come to attempt the route. Sometimes a line looks very straightforward but unexpected difficulties can turn you back; at other times your prediction of where the line should go and the difficulties to be encountered prove to be correct and you complete the ascent, with the bonus that you can then record and choose a name for your route.

Perhaps the best experience of all is when you select a line and set foot on the rock expecting formidable difficulties but find that the ascent is feasible. A famous line on the south face of Yosemite's Half Dome remained unattempted for years because it looked so hard and promised to need the full paraphernalia of multi-day big wall climbing. In the event, the climb went at 5.4 standard with a short section of 5.7 – a very modest grade. The pioneers dicovered that, instead of a long and arduous struggle, they in fact had a joyful romp up an astonishing ladder of holds across otherwise blank slabs.

In 1970 a group of friends and I were exploring the tremendous granite faces of Arctic Norway. Two of us had spotted a compelling groove line which led as straight as an arrow to the shapely summit of the Eidetind. It looked far too difficult but, despite completing a number of other climbs, our eyes were continually attracted to this line. Finally, we decided to make an attempt, more to get the idea out of our minds than in any real expectation of success. As we climbed, it rapidly became clear that the honey-coloured rock was irreproachable, in both its quality and its behaviour. Every time an obstacle such as a roof blocking the groove appeared, so would perfect holds to allow us to climb on. The climb was about 600m (1970ft) in length, of just the right difficulty to keep the outcome in doubt until the last moment and of outstanding quality throughout. As we sat on the summit watching the Arctic sun gradually slip down towards the Lofoten Islands, I could not imagine having a better climbing day anywhere.

Exploration is not always like this! Sometimes the rock is appallingly loose and unhelpful or the line simply peters out, forcing you back or onto an existing route. Also, the risks can be greater. We once completed a new climb which we called Guillotine because of an enormous and dangerously poised flake that we had to pass gingerly. This was not a climb that we recommended to other people.

World climbing

Climbing is a world-wide sport and you can find superb rock climbing in Thailand and Patagonia, Australia and Baltistan, Spain and South Africa. The popular climbing magazines regularly survey different areas and it is very enjoyable to sample different crags, different climates and different climbing cultures. Before you go, you can usually get hold of a guide book and map from one of the big specialist climbing shops in your own country, and it is then worth doing some homework on what you are likely to encounter. When you visit a totally new area in this way, as long as you do not breach any of the local codes of practice, I can virtually guarantee that you will find the local climbers tremendously helpful. Throughout the world, climbers think that their local crag is probably just about the best crag in the world, although they might generously allow it to come a good second to El Capitan. Just as many parents never tire of talking about their children, so these climbers will enthusiastically show you the delights (and horrors!) of their pet crag.

Recently, after a long drive across the desert, a friend and I arrived at the end of a dirt track which we hoped was leading to a climbing area called Owen's River Gorge. We were relieved to find someone who was immediately recognizable as a climber just loading a rucksack into his car. He eagerly spread guide books and topos on the front of his car and started enthusiastically telling us where to go and what to do. We were a little shell-shocked from the drive and perhaps my mind was wandering, but suddenly he shouted, 'Don't move!' I followed his eyes downward

9.1 Winter climbing.

just in time to see a large snake slithering inches from the toe of my san-
dals. This was the kind of excitement that I certainly would not get on
my home crag!

Winter climbing

Climbing in true winter conditions when snow and ice sheathe the rocks
is tremendously exciting. It has an elemental quality, a sense of struggle
against hostile nature that some people find irresistible. The days are
short, the conditions adverse, but your surroundings are magical and the
sense of achievement enormous.

If you already rock climb you will quickly learn the necessary techniques of winter climbing but it really is an entirely new sport. You will
need a whole new set of equipment (figure 9.1) – heavy boots, cram-
pons, ice-axes and specialist clothing – and you will have to master a
great many new techniques. What will transfer best from rock climbing
will be your knowledge of ropework and belaying, because the same

broad principles apply, although protection is generally poorer. The veneer of ice certainly affects the placing of equipment, belays must often be more dynamic than in rock climbing and you may well use specialist items such as pitons, ice-screws or 'dead men' (metal plates used as snow anchors); but the basic techniques will make complete sense to you.

Perhaps the hardest thing to learn is an appreciation of the tremendous severity of winter storms and the devastating effect of avalanches. Some people assume that avalanches only affect the very highest and most wintry of mountains. This is not the case and any mountain area that has drifting snow will, on occasions, present an avalanche risk – with winter climbers in the front line.

Alpine climbing

Many of my remarks about winter climbing apply with even more force to alpine climbing, but here there are the additional hazards of glacial crevasses, serac fall and stonefall. Alpine climbing is wonderful, but even on the easiest climbs you need to have an understanding of these special hazards.

When I was 17 I made my first ever visit to the French Alps. We set off to do a popular rock climb high on the Aiguille du Midi which is usually approached by cable-car. We could see the trail in the snow that previous climbers had followed to the foot of the climb, but it appeared to us to follow a ludicrously long dog-leg. With the ignorance of youth we headed off, unroped, across the glacier towards the foot of the climb. After about 300m (980ft) the snow beneath my feet gave way and I fell through a fragile snow bridge up to my armpits. My feet kicked above green depths below and not a few anxious moments followed while my partner uncoiled the rope and threw me a rescue loop. **Never** cross a snow-covered glacier without wearing a rope and knowing how to do a crevasse rescue, and **never** climb without a helmet where there may be any stonefall danger.

There are now some superb rock climbs, often with bolt protection, on isolated buttresses of high mountains. The approach will be through high mountain terrain with all its attendant hazards and you are always at the mercy of unexpected bad weather. Once on the rock, the techniques are entirely of a rock-climbing nature and the descents likely to be by abseil from fixed anchors.

Ask any climber and you will be told that climbing is quite simply the best sport there has ever been! Somewhere, the sun is just coming up on a crag of perfect rock, warming the holds and picking out tempting lines of possibility. Don't just sit there, get out your boots and go climbing!

Appendices

1 Useful addresses

Australia
Australian Sport Climbing
    Federation
GPO Box 3786
327 Sussex Street
Sydney NSW 2001

Austria
Verhand Alpiner Vereine
    Osterreichs
Bäckerstrasse 16/2
A-1010 Vienna

Belgium
Club Alpin Belge
rue de l'Aurore
19 B-1050 Brussels

Canada
Alpine Club of Canada
Box 2040
278 St Barbara's Terrace
Canmore T0l 0M0
Alberta

Fédération Québécoise de la
    Montagne
4545 avenue Pierre-de-Coubertin
CP 1000 Succursdale 'M'
Montreal
Quebec H1V 3R2

Denmark
Dansk Bjiergklub
Moelloparken 28, Brede
DK-2800 Lyngby

France
Fédération Française de la
    Montagne et de l'Escalade
16 rue Louis Dardenne
F-92170 Vanves

Germany
Deutscher Alpenverein
Von-Kahr Strasse 2–4
D-8099 Munich

Hong Kong
Hong Kong Mountaineering
    Union
Kowloon Central Post Office
Box 70837 Hong Kong

India
Indian Mountaineering
    Foundation
Benito Juarez Road
Anand Niketan
New Delhi 110021

Ireland
Irish Alpine Association
c/o AFAS
House of Sport
Longmile Road
Dublin 12

Italy
Club Alpino Italiano
Via E. Fonseca Pimentel 7
I-20127 Milan

Federazione Arrampicata Sportiva
    Italiana
Via Saluzzo 68
I-10125 Turin

Japan
Japan Mountaineering Association
Kishi Memorial Hall
Jinnan 1-1-1 Shibuya-ku
Tokyo 150

Netherlands
Koninklijke Nederlandse
    Alpenverenging
Postbus 19118
NL-3501 DC Utrecht

Nederlandse Klim- en Bergsport
    Bond
Postbus 19067
NL-3501 DB Utrecht

New Zealand
New Zealand Alpine Club
PO Box 3040
Wellington

Norway
Norges Klatreforbund
Norwegian Climbing Federation
Postboks 82
N-1351 Rud

Norsk Tindeklub
Postboks 8309 Hammersborg
N-0129 Oslo 1

South Africa
The Mountain Club of South
    Africa
97 Hatfield Street
Cape Town 8001

Switzerland
Club Alpin Suisse
Geschäftsstelle SAC
Helvetiaplatz 4
CH-3005 Berne

UK
British Mountaineering Council
177–179 Burton Road
West Didsbury
Manchester M20 2BB

USA
The American Alpine Club
710 10th Street
Golden
Colorado 80401

Abseil A friction-controlled descent down a rope.

Aerobic Muscles work aerobically when supplied with oxygen. They work anaerobically when starved of oxygen.

Aid climbing Climbing using direct physical assistance from equipment placed in the rock.

Anchor A rock feature or a piece of equipment placed in the rock to which a rope can be attached. A good anchor would be able to support a weight of 1 or 2 tonnes.

Arête An edge of rock like the outside corner of a house.

Arm–bar A hold created by wedging the forearm across a wide crack.

Ascender A mechanical device that grips a rope.

Back-and-foot A technique for climbing chimneys using opposed pressure between the back on one wall and the feet on the other. Back-and-knee is used similarly on narrower chimneys.

Bandolier A sling for carrying gear worn diagonally across the chest and shoulder.

Belay 1. An anchor.
2. The secure attachment of a climber to an anchor.
3. The protection given, via the rope, to a climber by their companion.

Belayer The person securing the rope of a moving climber to provide protection against a fall.

Bight The loop resulting when a rope is folded back upon itself.

Block An angular piece of rock detached from the main crag.

Bolt An anchor placed in the rock by drilling and secured mechanically or with adhesives.

Bouldering Climbing, usually without ropes, on short, problem climbs for training purposes.

Bridging Also called stemming. Straddling a groove or chimney with one foot on each wall.

Bucket *See* Jug.

Buildering As for bouldering but on buildings.

Camming device A mechanical device with springloaded cams that can provide an anchor in many types of crack.

Chain coil A method of coiling a rope into bag that permits very rapid uncoiling.

Chalk Light magnesium carbonate used on the hands to improve grip on difficult rock climbs.

COLEG POWYS - BRECON

Chicken-head A particularly well-formed spike of rock that provides an excellent handhold. (U.S.A.)

Chimney A fissure between about 30cm and 150cm (12in and 5ft) in width, with roughly parallel sides.

Chockstone A detached block or boulder which is jammed into a crack or chimney. This can occur naturally or by intention.

Cinching Threading a sling through itself to form a lark's foot around an object such as a spike.

Cirque, coire or **cwm** A bowl-shaped hollow on a mountain created by glacial action. It often contains crags.

Cold clip A convenient lower-off point at the top of a sport climb.

Corner A rock feature like the inside corner of a room. A groove with walls roughly at 90 degrees.

Couloir A gully particularly in alpine regions.

Cow's tail A short sling attached to the climber's harness to provide temporary attachment to an anchor.

Crack A fissure which might be from hairline thickness to about 30cm (12in) in width.

Crux The hardest section of a pitch or climb.

Delicate A climb where good balance and precise technique pay greater dividends than brute force.

Descender A friction device, most commonly used for abseiling.

Dihedral/Dièdre Another name for a corner or groove.

Down-climb To descend by climbing down rather than abseiling. On a multi-pitch climb. the most experienced climber would usually descend last, with protection from runners placed by the first person down.

Dyno A dynamic leap for a hold.

Deadman A metal plate which is used as an anchor in snow

Ectomorph A body-type, inclined to be tall and slender. Endomorphs tend to be short and stocky with mesomorphs somewhere between the two.

Extender A short, tape sling, equipped with two karabiners, most commonly used to provide a flexible link between the rope and the anchor of a running belay. Also called a 'quick draw'.

Fall factor A theoretical concept which gives an indication of the likely severity of the impact force following a fall. It is obtained by dividing the length of fall by the length of active rope holding that fall

Finger stacking Finger jamming with a bunch of fingers.

Fingerjam or **fingerlock** Placing the fingers just above a constriction in a crack and then wedging them in the constriction to create a hold.

Flake A generally flat sheet of rock which is separated by a small gap from the main crag

Flake crack The crack between a flake and the main crag. Often climbed by layback technique.

Flaking a rope Running a rope into random coils on the ground so that it can be taken up without tangling.

Free climbing Climbing with no direct assistance from equipment placed in the rock.

Glacis A slab of rock at such an easy angle that it can be walked up.

Glass reinforced plastic (GRP) Usually called fibreglass, a modern, strong material.

Groove A feature formed when two planes of rock meet to form an acute or obtuse angle. If they meet at an angle of 90 degrees, the groove would usually be referred to as a corner.

Gully A large chimney or groove that is usually a major drainage line.

Hand jam A hold created by jamming the hand in a crack.

Hand traverse A traverse on good hand holds but with poor or non-existent foot holds.

Harness, full body A harness that extends from the thighs to the shoulders and incorporates and combines both chest and sit-harnesses. *See also* Sit-harness

Hawser-laid A traditional construction of ropes using a helical arrangement of fibres.

Impact force The force developed in the belay system while a fall is being arrested.

Jam A generic term for any hold created by jamming fingers, hands, arms, knees or feet.

Jug Short for jug handle. A particularly positive and good handhold. Also called a 'bucket'. (U.S.A.)

Karabiner A strong spring-loaded metal clip.

Kernmantel A modern rope construction, using parallel fibres of a synthetic material within a woven sheath.

Kevlar A modern synthetic fibre used to make ropes which are very strong but have very limited elasticity.

Kilonewton A unit of force. 19.8kN = 1 Kpond (approx).

Kilopond The force due to gravity acting on a weight of 1000kg (2200lb). For practical purposes it is identical to 1000kg weight.

Knot *bowline* A traditional knot for forming a loop in any rope. It does not jam but can become accidentally untied.

clove hitch In climbing, this traditional hitch is used to secure a rope to a karabiner.

double fisherman's Used to join two ropes of similar diameter.

figure-of-eight A versatile knot, most commonly used to form the loop which attaches a climber to the end of the climbing rope.

grapevine Another name for the double fisherman's knot.

Italian hitch A friction hitch used by passing the rope through a screwgate karabiner. It can be used for abseiling or lowering.

klemheist A simple form of prusik knot used for ascending ropes.

lark's foot A simple hitch threading a sling back through itself for attachment to a piton or spike. It is convenient but weakens the sling considerably.

Munter hitch Another name for the Italian hitch. A friction hitch.

overhand The simplest of all knots.

reef Should be confined to tying up parcels. Not a secure joining knot.

stopper Any knot used to prevent another knot from untying accidentally. The fisherman's knot or the overhand knot are most commonly used.

tape or water A knot used for joining climbing tape. It is a rethreaded overhand knot

Lay away A handhold that is used to best effect by the climber leaning out to the side of it.

Laybacking Climbing a feature, such as a corner crack, by opposed pressure between the hands pulling and the feet pushing.

Leader The person who climbs first up a pitch.

Locking off Holding the body weight stationary on a bent arm to allow the other arm to reach upwards.

Mantelshelf A strenuous manoeuvre, allowing the climber to move up onto a narrow ledge, without assistance from holds on the wall above.

Multi-pitch A climb that is divided into more than one pitch.

Nubbin A tiny hold or rugosity.

Nut A generic term for any shaped piece of metal jammed in a crack to form an anchor. Nuts are threaded with rope or wire slings.

Off-width A crack of an uncomfortable width, too wide for hand jamming and too narrow for chimneying.

Overhang An area of rock steeper than its surroundings and somewhat steeper than the vertical.

Pinch grip A hold that is used by pinching as one would grip a drawer handle.

Pitch A convenient section of a climb between two stances.

Piton An eyed metal spike that is driven into cracks to provide an anchor.

Prusik knot A specific knot that can grip a rope but the name is now used generically for any knot that does this.

Prusik loop A sling made of relatively thin kernmantel line, which is particularly suitable for forming a prusik knot.

Prusiking Climbing a rope by using prusik knots or ascenders.

Quick-draw Another name for an extender.

Racking Arranging equipment in a logical manner at the start of a pitch.

Rand An area of rubber extending from the sole of a rock boot over the foot and heel.

Rappelling Another name for abseiling.

Rock intelligence The ability to solve rock climbing problems quickly and effectively.

Roll-ups A training technique for developing finger strength.

Roof An overhang where the underside is almost horizontal.

Rope: *active* The rope between the belayer and a moving climber.

    dead The slack rope that is not the active rope.

    double Climbing with two ropes.

    dynamic A rope with considerable elasticity and energy absorption. Climbing ropes are dynamic ropes.

    full A rope suitable for use as a single rope.

    half A rope suitable for use as a double rope.

    live Another name for active rope.

    single Climbing with a single rope between leader and second.

    static A rope which has little elasticity and therefore limited energy absorption. Not suitable as a main climbing rope

Roping, bottom A belaying system on single-pitch climbs, where the belayer stays on the ground and the rope passes through a pulley arrangement at the top of the climb.

Roping, top An arrangement on single pitch climbs, where the belayer sits at the top of a climb and drops the rope down to the second.

Runner Short for running belay. An intermediate anchor on a pitch, intended to reduce the length of a potential fall by a leader.

Screwgate A form of locking karabiner.

Second A person who has not led a pitch, following it with protection from the rope.

Serac A large, detached block of ice formed on a glacier.

Side pulls Holds that are most effectively used for sideways pulls.

Single pitch A climb that can be completed in one pitch.

Sit-harness A harness consisting of a waist belt and combined legloops. *See also* Harness, full body.

Slab A face of rock, generally between about 40 and 70 degrees from the horizontal.

Sling Any loop of rope or tape.

Smear A technique to use poor footholds by putting the maximum area of the boot sole in contact with the rock.

Snaplink A non-locking karabiner.

Solo climbing Climbing alone and generally unroped.

Spike A rock feature like a small pinnacle.

Sprag A hold formed by opposing pressure between thumb and fingers.

Stance The starting point and finishing point of a pitch on a multi-pitch climb. Preferably it is on a ledge and is a point from which a belay is given to the other climber.

Stemming Another name for bridging.

Strenuous Climbing that puts great demands on strength

Stuff-sac A soft nylon bag with a drawstring.

Threading Passing a sling or the rope around a chockstone or natural thread.

Topo A topological diagram of a climb.

Traversing Climbing predominantly sideways.

Undercling Using opposing pressure to allow the use of 'downward-pointing' holds. A downward-pointing hold.

Index